AIMING HIGH

To our families and friends

AIMING HIGH

Raising the Attainment of Pupils from Culturally Diverse Backgrounds

Marie Parker-Jenkins
Des Hewitt
Simon Brownhill
Tania Sanders

P·CP

Paul Chapman
Publishing

Paul Chapman Publishing
A SAGE Publications Company
1 Oliver's Yard
55 City Road
London EC1Y 1SP

SAGE Publications Inc
2455 Teller Road
Thousand Oaks, California 91320

SAGE Publications India Pvt Ltd
B 1/I 1 Mohan Cooperative Industrial Area
Mathura Road
New Delhi 110 044

SAGE Publications Asia-Pacific Pte Ltd
33 Pekin Street #02-01
Far East Square
Singapore 048763

Library of Congress Control Number: 2007927216

A catalogue record for this book is available from the British Library

ISBN 978-1-4129-2938-7
ISBN 978-1-4129-2939-4 (pbk)

Typeset by Pantek Arts Ltd, Maidstone, Kent
Printed in Great Britain by Cromwell Press Ltd, Trowbridge, Wiltshire
Printed on paper from sustainable resources

CONTENTS

'Asian' – used generically to include people of South East Asian heritage, for example Indian, Pakistani, Bangladeshi and Kashmiri.

asylum seeker – someone who has crossed an international border and is seeking safety or protection in another country. This involves awaiting a government decision as to whether they can remain.

attainment – the personal achievement of pupils and their acquisition of knowledge as measured in an academic environment and evidenced by performance in formal tests, such as the Statutory Test Framework and GCSE (QCA 1999).

bilingual student – a student who has access to, or needs to use, two or more languages at home and school. It does not imply fluency in the languages and includes students who are beginning to learn English (Rutter 2001).

Black – a term used increasingly since the 1970s to refer to people of African, Caribbean, mixed/race or dual heritage, and those of South Asian descent.

class – social class refers to the socio-economic position of people in society, their financial situation and their access to public services.

community – a group of people with shared values, ethnic, religious and/or linguistic background.

culture – ideas, techniques and habits which are passed on by one generation to another.

cultural racism – dislike or discrimination against someone on the basis of their culture.

development – in learning this can be conceived as the child's adaptation to his or her environment. Children develop physically, emotionally, cognitively and socially, and some would argue that children also develop at a moral or spiritual level.

dual heritage – the possession of two cultural backgrounds.

EMAG – Ethnic Minority Achievement Grant

English as an Additional Language – pupils who speak English as an additional language (EAL).

ethnicity – relates to a person's place of birth or historical place of origin, symbolized by visible signifiers such as colour, dress, lifestyle or birthplace allegiance.

Eurocentric – placing White Europeans and/or Americans as the norm and the sole contributors to such things as scientific discovery.

Every Child Matters – a new government approach (DfES 2006c) to the well-being of children and young people from birth to age 19. Organizations that provide services to children are required to work together in terms of policies and strategies to improve outcomes for children.

gender – refers to the social meaning of what it is to be male or female rather than biological characteristics.

Gypsy – a term originating in Egypt which refers to a range of different ethnic and cultural groups who live a nomadic lifestyle.

Islamophobia – hostility towards Islam and fear and/or dislike of Muslims.

Local Authority (LA) – local authority, formerly known as LEA (Local Education Authority), legally responsible for the management of public affairs at a local level.

madrassah – religious or mosque school.

mentoring – to guide, support and give advice.

minority ethnic group – people who are identifiably different, sometimes through language, accent, religion or dress, from the majority ethnic population.

mixed race – refers to people who have more than one racial origin, now more commonly replaced by the term 'dual heritage'.

parent/carer – someone who has the legal responsibility for a child, aged 0–18. Legal responsibility varies according to case orders placed by the court and is mostly a matter of joint responsibility with the local authority.

practitioners – teachers, trainees, teaching assistants (namely adults working in the classroom with pupils).

racism – consists of conduct or words or practices which disadvantage or advantage people because of their colour, culture or ethnic origin. It may be overt or subtle, and underpinned by power.

RAISE project – funded by the Yorkshire Forward regional development agency to reduce and remove inequalities concerning the achievement of young people of Pakistani and Kashmiri heritage.

refugee – someone who has had to leave his/her own country and who is afraid to return there owing to a fear of being persecuted for reasons of race, religion, nationality or membership of a social or political group.

religious literacy – an awareness of the diversity of religious groups in society and of the importance of religion as a sense of identity.

Roma – gypsies originating from Eastern Europe.

Travellers – people who travel around the country for economic reasons or as a lifestyle choice.

ABOUT THE AUTHORS

Marie Parker-Jenkins is Professor of Research in Education at the University of Derby, researching issues of social justice with particular reference to 'race' and ethnicity. Before having an academic career in the UK, she taught in Bermuda, Canada and Australia where she obtained practical knowledge of teaching children from culturally diverse backgrounds. She is the author of over 100 publications including books, reports and journal articles. Her current research focuses on the expansion of religious schools, particularly those based on an Islamic and Jewish ethos; and in her consultancy capacity, she runs workshops on citizenship and identity.

Dr Des Hewitt has taught from Year 5 through to doctoral students over the last year! As Assistant Head of Teacher Education he has principal responsibility for managing the initial teacher education of Primary teachers. His research and teaching encompass Primary English, Primary Modern Foreign Languages, English as an Additional Language, e-learning and the development of self-regulated learning. He has published papers in respect of teacher education, the role of schools facing challenging circumstances, and assessment for learning in higher education institutions. Des is currently working on a book about the use of learning strategies in schools (*Understanding Effective Learning*). Future projects include the development of out of school learning with the National Forest and the development of independent learning in Early Years settings in a professional development cluster in the East Midlands.

Simon Brownhill (MEd) is a Senior Lecturer in Initial Teacher Education at the University of Derby, co-ordinating the PGCE 3–7 course and the Foundation Subjects for the PGCE and BEd. Prior to this he worked for a number of years in primary schools, particularly in the early years. With a varied experience of teaching children in a range of Key Stage One, Two and Three settings, Simon continues to work actively with children in primary schools on a voluntary basis. His teaching and research interests include working with learners from culturally diverse backgrounds, developing creativity in the classroom, and effective learning and teaching in English. A long-term interest in effective behaviour management has led to Simon writing a number of practical and academic books about this topic. He is currently studying for his Doctorate in Education (EdD) which examines the male role model in early years education.

Tania Sanders (MEd) was appointed as the Primary Achievement Co-ordinator for the Ethnic Minority Achievement Service (The Access Service) for Derby City LA in 2000. Since then her work has involved teaching and supporting asylum seeker and refugee pupils. Tania also plans and delivers professional development for teachers and teaching assistants. One recent successful initiative has been the co-ordination of a cross-agency group that involves an educational psychologist, a nurse practitioner, a mental health worker and a university lecturer looking at the emotional well-being of asylum seeker and refugee pupils. This collaborative approach to training delivery has been recognized by the National Children's Bureau. Tania is also one of the authors of the Raise Project, 2004 (raising attainment in multi-ethnic and multi-faith schools with particular regard to Muslim pupils of Pakistani and Kashmiri heritage). Tania's chapter looks at the impact of the Talking Partners Project on raising the attainment of EAL pupils in one Derby city school. In her spare time Tania is an ardent rock-climber and has climbed in the Alps, the Dolomites and has made an attempt on the Old Man of Hoy, Orkney.

FOREWORD

There is a growing body of literature highlighting improvements in the educational attainment of Black and minority ethnic pupils in compulsory education. However, it is clear that gaps in attainment levels between Black and minority ethnic pupils and others remain. At the same time, a raft of government initiatives has been created to specifically address this situation. Current government proposals are in the shape of the Education and Inspection Act 2006. According to the Department for Education and Skills, the overarching aim of this legislation is to ensure that "every child in every in school in every community gets the education they need to enable them to fulfil their potential".

At a time when only one third of newly qualified teachers in the UK report that they feel prepared to meet the needs of pupils from Black and minority ethnic communities, it would seem that teachers and schools also need support in their work with pupils from culturally diverse backgrounds.

This book is a valuable addition to the literature describing how practical school and classroom initiatives can assist Black and minority ethnic pupils raise their attainment. The focus on a variety of "culturally diverse bckgrounds" is particularly helpful. Examples are drawn from both primary and secondary schools. These are of particular use in assisting practitioners in schools with either new arrivals and/or established minority ethnic groups.

The main body of the book provides a series of scenarios and practical guidelines for teachers, teaching assistants and policy makers in schools who are both supporting new pupils holding refugee/asylum status and are also handling the issue of Black male underachievement and Gypsy/Traveller children. The scenarios presented and questions posed are thought provoking and valuable for both existing teachers and those working towards Qualified Teacher Status.

Many suggestions are made with regard to parental involvement and that of the wider local community. Primary teachers/trainees and secondary teachers/trainees would benefit considerably from the practical training advice contained in the book.

Cecile Wright
Nottingham Trent University

ACKNOWLEDGEMENTS

Our research for this book has involved discussion and correspondence with a number of people who have all played a role in providing us with invaluable information and informing our practice. We would like, therefore, to acknowledge these individuals and organizations.

For the purposes of the study we conducted research in successful schools which could be described as 'attaining schools', and our thanks go to:

Barry Day and the staff at Greenwood Dale Community School, Sneinton, Nottingham;

David Nichols and the staff at Littleover Community School, Derby.

In terms of local authority support we were assisted by:

Catherine Conchar, Equalities Officer, Nottingham City Local Authority;

Lorna Simpson and Maureen Rhule, Advisory Support Teachers for African Caribbean Learners, Access Service, Derby City Local Authority;

Nigel Groom, Head of the Traveller Service, Derby City Local Authority.

We also wish to acknowledge the Teacher Development Agency in supporting our earlier project work (2002–4), much of which underpins this publication.

We were very keen that a variety of practitioners gave input to our manuscript as it evolved and we wish to thank the following who acted as reviewers for the book: Maxine Bull, St Chad's Infant School; Judith Lloyd Williams, Sinfin Primary School; and Dr Musharaf Hussain, head teacher, the Islamic School, Nottingham.

Within the University of Derby, we would like to acknowledge the specialist advice of Khrissey Hartley, Widening Participation Project Leader; Lyn Senior, Post-Compulsory Education and Training Manager; Jane Keeling, Subject Advisor: Education; the research assistance of Sarah Dyke and Jane Lyon; and the secretarial assistance of Selina McCarthy.

We are also grateful to Jude Bowen at Sage Publications for on-going support of the book.

The foreward was provided by Cecile Wright, Professor of Sociology, Nottingham Trent University, to whom we are particularly indebted.

While a number of people and organizations have thus been consulted over issues contained in the book, the opinions expressed are our own; likewise any errors or omissions.

Marie Parker-Jenkins, University of Derby
Des Hewitt, University of Derby
Simon Brownhill, University of Derby
Tania Sanders, Derby City LA
2007.

We have shaped the book's chapters around a number of themes or strands within social diversity. Chapter 1 serves as an introduction to the book and the context in which practitioners are responding to meeting the needs of learners from culturally diverse backgrounds. Chapter 2 provides discussion and strategies for responding to the changing nature of diversity in the classroom, with particular reference to the needs of refugee and asylum seeker children and induction for new arrivals.

The focus then moves in Chapter 3 to supporting bilingual learners with recognition of the importance of the home language and strategies to support learning in an additional language. Discussion in Chapter 4 refers to the issue of raising the attainment of 'Black boys', particularly those groups which government reports state are under-performing academically, namely Black Caribbean and Black African, and Pakistani and Bangladeshi boys (DfES 2006a). Here we highlight identity issues based on ethnicity, gender and social class, and consider multiple or mixed senses of identity.

Of all the groups under-performing academically, Gypsy, Roma and Traveller children in the UK are the lowest achievers, particularly at Secondary level (DfES 2006a). In Chapter 5 we look at the work being done to respond to this group of learners. Part of the success in working with minority groups is also to engage with parents and in Chapter 6 we look particularly at how we can involve and work with parents and the community as partners in supporting children's learning.

Overall, our aim is to move beyond theory and the rehearsing of social justice and underachievement debates, and to offer practitioners practical suggestions and activities to help raise the academic attainment of their pupils. Whilst much of the discussion has implication as good practice for all pupils, there is particular reference to pupils from culturally diverse backgrounds due to the under-attainment of specific minority ethnic groups. We are advocating an inclusive approach to make sure that every pupil can achieve academically, and that practitioners develop policies and structures which allow for all learner groups to have the best opportunities to succeed.

CHAPTER 1

Introduction

> All children and young people should be able to achieve their potential, whatever their ethnic and cultural background and whichever school they attend. (*Aiming High*, DfES 2003a, p.4)

In the national and political context, raising the attainment of culturally diverse pupils continues to be an area of importance. This is especially true for trainee teachers and trainers who have to ensure that the standards relating to the inclusion of minority ethnic groups are met (TTA 2002). Academic under-performance leads to disenfranchisement of particular groups in our society and OFSTED reports have focused increasingly on this issue, noting that among the characteristics of effective Local Authority (LA) management is an acceptance by schools that support for raising the attainment of pupils from minority ethnic backgrounds is integral to the pursuit of higher education and part of school improvement. Government reports have also emphasized the need to develop appropriate strategies to raise the attainment of all pupils (OFSTED 1996a).

This book is set within the context of government concern over the under-achievement of minority ethnic groups, particularly those from Black Caribbean, Black African, Pakistani and Bangladeshi backgrounds (Pupil Level Annual Schools Census, DfES 2006a). Recent statistics confirm that these groups of pupils generally have lower levels of attainment than other ethnic groups across all the Key Stages (DfES 2006b). We are a team of researchers from academic, school and LA backgrounds, working in the field of supporting diversity in the classroom, and we are writing this book to help meet the need to raise the achievement of pupils from culturally diverse backgrounds.

Setting the historical context

Concern over the experience and underachievement of minority ethnic groups is not new and indeed has been documented over the last few decades (Coard 1971; Troyna 1986; Gaine 1987; Wright 1992; Gillborn 1996). Similarly, the Parekh Report (2000) emphasized that in a multicultural, multifaith society there needs to be 'respect for deep moral difference'. Factors associated with attainment, for example, have also been identified by a number of writers, such as Callender

(1997), Wright (1992), Fuller (1980) and Mirza (1992). More recently, concern has been expressed over the positioning of 'Black boys' (Sewell 1996, 2007), and indeed boys in general have emerged high on the political agenda because of their consistent under-achievement at all stages of education (DfES 2006a; TES 2006).

The OFSTED report 'Managing Support for the Attainment of Pupils from Minority Ethnic Groups' (2001) noted that although there were pockets of good practice, there were still certain minority ethnic groups which were under-performing, notably Black Caribbean and those of Asian heritage, Pakistani and Bangladeshis. The report also noted that many schools were developing a range of strategies both within and outside the classroom to try and rectify the situation. It is within this aspect of the complex issue of under-achievement that this book is concerned.

The racially motivated murder of Stephen Lawrence (MacPherson Inquiry Report 1999) and the recommendations which followed provided impetus within race equality work for change, as detailed in the Race Relations (Amendment) Act 2000. Importantly, this inquiry helped inform the framework of the Commission for Race Equality's framework *Learning for All* (2000) which has been circulated to all schools and which places a duty on a wide range of public authorities, amongst them schools, to promote race equality. Similarly, the government's 'Respect' initiative carries with it an expectation that schools will demonstrate an understanding of and be sensitive to cultural diversity in the classroom (see www.respect.gov.uk 2006). How this works in practice, and what the implications for teachers and trainees are, form the basis of discussion throughout this book.

The situation is not static and the nature of cultural diversity in the classroom is constantly changing. Under-attainment among minority ethnic groups encompasses a range of different groups with different levels of academic success and therefore different needs in terms of policy and practice. For the purpose of this book we will be highlighting 'good practice' strategies in raising academic attainment with regard to Black African and Caribbean boys, Pakistani and Bangladeshi boys, pupils who speak English as an additional language, the UK's Gypsy, Roma and Traveller pupils and Refugee–Asylum Seeker children. We will also be reaffirming the belief that 'Every Child Matters' (DfES 2006c), and that they should be supported in making a contribution to society and achieving economic well-being.

The 2005 riots in Paris of disaffected youth, many of whom were from minority ethnic backgrounds, highlighted the fact that there are significant groups which feel they are discriminated against in society and that their ethnic origins reduce their chances of equal opportunity and meaningful employment (*Guardian* 2005, 2006). This is a salutary lesson to others that now more than ever policy makers and practitioners need to look at issues of social inclusion and fairness with respect to the treatment of minority groups in schools. Press coverage regarding asylum seekers in this country (*Times* 2007), and controversy over the wearing of the veil by Muslim women here and in France and Holland (*Independent* 2006a, 2006b) help to generate a climate of opinion which is negative towards some communities. This goes towards emphasizing the importance of schools providing a welcoming environment where pupils can feel safe, secure and settled, and where they can be in a position to achieve academically.

This, then, is intended as a highly practical book which will support practitioners in raising the attainment of pupils, especially those from culturally diverse backgrounds. We draw on data from England and Wales, recognizing devolution, but also acknowleging that notions of community, ethnicity and identity have implications across the British Isles and beyond. We attempt to filter the theory and link it with practice. Throughout each chapter we define and clarify key issues and concepts, and provide discussion relevant to Qualified Teacher Status requirements to ensure that all pupils are achieving their true potential (TTA 2002). Practical strategies, activities, bullet-pointed information and illustrations are used to explore academic attainment across all three phases of Foundation, Primary and Secondary level (Foundation level is working towards and attaining the Early Learning goals which allow pupils to access the National Curriculum at Level 1). There is also a focus on the social and emotional aspects of learning which affect motivation, quality of learning and attainment. Two central questions are raised throughout the book:

- What does the school need to know, and need to do?

- What does the classroom teacher or teaching assistant need to do?

The focus is practical rather than theoretical in terms of lesson activities, improving teaching skills, case studies, vignettes, professional reflection activities and identifying strategies to raise attainment. Crucially, the issues of challenging racism and Islamophobia, and of providing equality of opportunity, are embedded in each chapter. Campaigners for reform of race relations legislation have lobbied for 'cultural racism' as well as 'colour racism' to be included in our understanding of discrimination (Modood 2003, 2006 et al). Both race and religion are markers of personal and cultural identity and within the recent Racial and Religious Hatred Act 2006 'the criminalizing of incitement to religious hatred' acknowledges the need to respect religious sensibilities. As such we are encouraging readers to be 'religiously literate' and to have an awareness of the ways in which religion affects people's values and identity (Richardson and Wood 2004). Teachers need to demonstrate an understanding of cultural and religious difference, for there is no 'quick fix' or 'one size-fits-all' solution to the challenge of responding to diversity in the classroom, and in this book we encourage teachers to find out and think through for themselves and their own practice what strategies are most useful in their work in the classroom.

We have endeavoured throughout the book to signal the dynamic nature of cultural diversity in schools, and we have tried to provide definition and explanation of current terms together with the recognition that language in this area is dynamic, and that practitioners need to be open to constantly reviewing and if necessary refining their terms in the light of new groups arriving and new understandings of language.

Key terms and definitions

For the purpose of this book, it is important to set out the key terms and explain the way in which they are used throughout the discussion. A glossary is provided with a range of terms used, but the following represent the central terms of discussion which require definition and explanation at the outset:

'Asian' is used generically to include those pupils of South East Asian heritage, for example, Indian, Pakistani, Bangladeshi and Kashmiri. However, the term has been criticized because it ignores the huge differences in culture within these diverse groups (Modood et al. 1997).

'Attainment' is defined in terms of the personal achievement of pupils. The terms 'attainment', 'achievement' and 'performance' are all used interchangeably in the literature and in professional practice, but we are using the term 'attainment' to denote the acquisition of knowledge as measured in an academic environment. Within educational circles this is often evidenced by performance in formal tests such as the Statutory Test framework and at GCSE (QCA 1999). Achievement means different things in different schools, when measured for example in terms of social integration or linguistic progress (Wrigley 2000), and attainment may be low but performance is developing. Similarly, the Teaching and Learning Research Programme has focused on valuable forms of learning, such as the process of learning, self-assessment of learning and unintended learning outcomes (see ESRC, www.tlrp.org).

'Black' has been used increasingly since the 1970s to refer to people of African, Caribbean, mixed race or dual heritage, and those of South Asian descent, to define their sense of oppression and marginalization (Brah 1992). As such, 'Black' is used generically to include pupils of African Caribbean background and those of dual heritage or mixed race.

'Every Child Matters' (DfES 2006c) is a new approach to the well-being of children and young people from birth to age 19. Organizations that provide services to children are required to work together in terms of policies and strategies to improve outcomes for children. The government aim is for every child to be healthy, to stay safe, enjoy and achieve, to make a positive contribution and achieve economic well-being.

'Minority ethnic' or 'ethnic minority' are terms of convenience. Both are used to refer to groups of people who are identifiably different – sometimes through language, accent, religion or dress – to the ethnic majority (Dadzie 2000). Sometimes the differences are barely apparent. The movement away from 'ethnic minority', which infers a kind of marginalization, to that of 'minority ethnic' suggests the inclusion of all groups in society, visible or non-visible in terms of skin colour or ethnicity.

'Strategies' are activities in the educational process which include: teaching, planning, and assessment, managing other adults, and working with outside agencies.

Standards for Qualified Teacher Status

At the time of writing all qualified teachers must reach certain minimum standards in England, as part of their initial training. These are frequently called Qualified Teacher Status (QTS) standards. The first standards were published in 1998, new standards were outlined in 2002 and another revision is to take place in September 2007. Given the changes that are about to be made, we have decided not to outline a map of the current standards to the issues as they are dealt with by this book.

All trainee teachers should, however, find this book useful as it will help them to understand the following skills, knowledge and understanding, which have been taken from the current list of QTS standards. These require that a teacher:

- Recognizes and responds effectively to equal opportunities issues as they arise in the classroom, which includes challenging stereotyped views, and also bullying or harassment, following relevant policies and procedures.

- Respects pupils' social, cultural, linguistic, religious and ethnic backgrounds, establishing a purposeful learning environment where diversity is valued and pupils feel secure and confident.

- Understands how pupils' learning can be affected by physical, intellectual, linguistic, social, cultural and emotional development.

- Is able to support those who are learning English as an additional language, with the help of an experienced teacher where appropriate.

- With the help of experience, can identify the levels of attainment of those pupils learning English as an additional language, beginning to analyse the language demands and learning activities in order to a provide a cognitive challenge as well as language support.

Good practice starts from an understanding that the welcoming and care of asylum seeker and refugee children are whole-school issues. A great deal can be done by schools to provide appropriate and welcoming induction procedures which involve parents as partners in this process. The classroom teacher today has to respond to the concept of diversity in its widest sense, with the arrival of children from many parts of the world. To assist in this work multi-agency cooperation and use of local communities as a resource help provide support for practitioners and need to be seen as part of the process of continuing professional development.

CHAPTER 2

Induction for new arrivals

This chapter looks at:

- defining terminology

- the changing nature of diversity in the classroom

- the importance of induction for new arrivals

- home and community involvement

- working with other professionals

- bilingual learners

- academic attainment

- a checklist for an induction programme.

A newly qualified teacher in school reached the end of the register in his very first session:

'Shakil M ?'

(No reply.)

'Shakil M ?'

(No reply.)

'Sir, he's just come to England and doesn't speak English.'

The induction of new arrivals is an important issue for all teachers, and as this true incident demonstrates, concerns newly qualified as well as experienced teachers.

Throughout the country many schools have admitted asylum seeker and refugee pupils, and in one Midlands primary school, for example, 30 Sudanese children arrived for admission on one Monday morning. What follows are the strategies to support new arrivals which experienced teachers commonly cite as being important in the induction of new arrivals.

Defining terminology

Before we discuss aspects of accommodating the educational needs of asylum seeker and refugee children, it is important to clarify the distinction between the two groups, and the different legal positions they hold in trying to settle and be educated in a country.

■ A refugee refers to someone who has had to leave his or her own country and who is afraid to return there, 'owing to a well-founded fear of being persecuted for reasons of race, religion, nationality, membership of a particular social or political group' (*United Nations Convention Relating to the Status of Refugees* 1951).

■ An asylum seeker is someone who has crossed an international border and is seeking safety or protection in another country. In the UK, asylum seekers are refugees who have claimed asylum and are awaiting a Home Office decision as to whether they can stay here (The Refugee Council and Save the Children 2001).

■ EU Accession states – in 2003 the member states of the European Union agreed on the admission of ten new states to the Union. The new members joined 1 May 2004. New arrivals include Poland, Latvia and the Czech Republic. The accession states of Bulgaria and Romania took place in 2007.

Under the European Convention on Human Rights and Fundamental Freedoms 1949 (see www.hri.org/docs/ECHR50.html) which has now been incorporated into domestic law (Human Rights Act 1998), there is 'a right to education' for all people within a country's jurisdiction (see Article 2, Protocol 1). Added to this is the stipulation that in regard to the education provided, the state shall respect the 'religious and philosophical convictions of parents'.

The educational entitlement extends to all children residing in a region, whether temporarily or permanently, and local authorities are required to accommodate and respond to their needs.

The changing nature of diversity in the classroom

Since April 2000, the Home Office has operated a system of dispersal for asylum seeker pupils and there are now many primary and secondary schools that have received new arrivals for the first time (OFSTED 2003). By contrast, there are schools in which there are existing targeted pupils with English as an Additional Language (EAL), and the need for additional support for asylum seeker and refugee pupils has put a great deal of pressure on local authority central peripatetic teams and school-based Ethnic Minority Achievement Grant support staff.

Huge diversity exists among the various groups of children joining British schools, such as those from Albania, Ecuador and Bolivia (Rutter 2001) and from Africa particularly, for example, those from the Congo, Zimbabwe, Sudan and Somalia, and practitioners need to be well equipped to respond to this cultural change.

Successful practice suggests using school assemblies, and religious and cultural festivals, to raise awareness of the cultural backgrounds of the newly arrived asylum seeker/refugee pupils. Displays and labels can mirror the different languages of the school and time can be given in

Personal, Social and Health Education (PSHE) to explore work on citizenship. A useful booklet, for example, has been produced by Tower Hamlets Language Support Service entitled 'Somali Children in our Schools' and contains sections on the geography, history, language, religion and educational system of Somalia (Naidoo 2002). The Refugee Council has also produced many resources to give teachers and pupils a fuller understanding of the changing nature of cultural diversity (www.refugeecouncil.org.uk).

Activities – Diversity in the classroom

How many asylum seekers/refugees are there in your city/school?

How many languages are spoken in your city/school?

Which religions are represented in your school?

How do you show that all languages spoken in your school are valued?

How is religious diversity celebrated in your school/classroom?

Implications for practice

- Use interpreters where necessary – contact your local Ethnic Minority Achievement Service.

- Access dual language resources – available in 47 different languages (www.mantralingua.com).

- Promote the use of the mother tongue – classroom displays should reflect the languages of the classroom and it is helpful to have story books, bilingual dictionaries and tapes in relevant languages.

Understanding the importance of induction for new arrivals

One of the main points raised in the OFSTED (2003) report is the need to have an effective admissions/induction procedure in place in schools. It notes that asylum seeker and refugee pupils arrive at different times throughout the year and consequently enrolment and induction need to be handled in a sensitive way. Some schools have decided to designate certain days for admissions in order to give the children and parents particular attention. This also allows time for interpreters to be notified and to be present at the enrolment, thereby aiding effective communication and a smooth transition.

The report also makes clear that successful induction must involve parents in order that they are informed about the education of their children in this country, and are provided with details about such things as free school meals, assemblies, PE and the timing of the school day.

Many schools have made information packs for parents including services in the local area, and in some cases these packs have also been translated into the languages of the newly arriving asylum seeker and refugee families. Similarly, some LAs have encouraged schools to make videos of their schools, classrooms and staff with the dialogue in relevant languages. One LA in the North of England, for example, has produced a brochure for asylum seeker and refugee parents translated into six languages. It contains a list of all schools, information on supplementary schools in the area, a directory of voluntary organizations, National Health Service information, and a welcome leaflet from the police (Manchester City LA 2001).

One of the most comprehensive packs has been produced by Bolloten and Spafford (2003) for schools in the London Borough of Newham and is entitled 'Guidance – Managing Mid-phase Pupil Admissions'. We highlight the main strategies from this resource on pages 10 and 11, and ask you to consider the implications for your own practice.

Working with other professionals

Working with other agencies can assist schools to deal with some of the various issues that refugee children have to face. One of the key issues emerging from the texts that we reviewed for this book is that teachers need to be sensitive to the fact that newly arrived asylum seeker and refugee children may have suffered from experiences which greatly impact on their ability to make satisfactory academic progress (Baker 1983, Dyregor 1991, Furedi 1997, Rutter 1994).

For some asylum seeker and refugee families there can be medical, psychological and legal concerns and a multi-agency approach made up of, for example, health, social services and education professionals ensures best use of the demands on time, professional skills and resources, and can provide school practitioners with the support they need (Spafford and Bolloten 2001).

Recent professional development has been offered by the Refugee Council on the emotional well-being of asylum seeker and refugee pupils (see www.refugeecouncil.org.uk).

Activities: – Responding to New Arrivals

A family has just arrived in your area. The father is still in the country of origin – his whereabouts are unknown. This country is suffering from a civil war in what was the former Soviet Union. There are three children with the mother – a girl of 2 years, a boy of 6 years and another boy aged 10. The family speak little English, except for the elder boy. The elder boy and his mother have first-hand experience of the brutalities of civil war and both have been emotionally scarred by this.

The mother would like her elder children to resume their education in your primary school as soon as possible.

Using the chart on page 11, consider how the listed professionals might support this family.

Strategies for working with newly arrived asylum seeker and refugee children

- Involve children in making the school welcoming and supporting the setting process, e.g. creating a Welcome Book.

- Make use of a buddy system' which is monitored, evaluated, and provides recognition for the 'buddy'.

- Recognize the period of adjustment that some children may need, e.g. allow a 'silent period' during the settling-in process.

- Ensure newly arrived children have appropriate time and space to share their background and experiences of schooling elsewhere.

- Discuss routines and rules to encourage familiarity with the school.

- Use the curriculum to explore the experience of loss and displacement

Activity

How do you welcome new children into the school mid-phase?

How do you ensure they become familiar with the school and its routines?

How do you involve children in making new pupils feel welcome?

How do you use the children's experiences as part of learning?

Implications for your practice

-

-

-

Source: Teacher Development Agency

Consider how the following professionals might support this family

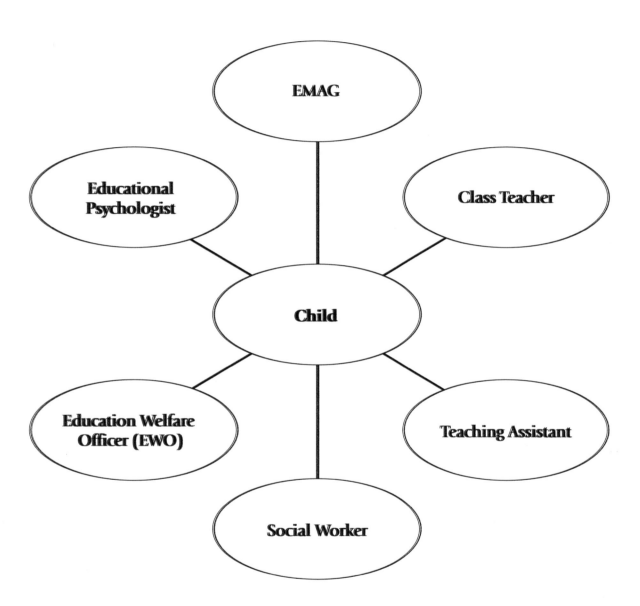

Bilingual learners

In the DfES report *Aiming High: Raising the Achievement of Minority Ethnic Pupils* (DfES 2003a), acknowledgement is made of the importance of recognizing and valuing the home languages of all new arrivals. The document states that children should be encouraged to maintain and develop their home languages. Research by Cummins (2003) highlights how bilingualism is of positive benefit to cognitive development. This point is also illustrated by work taking place in schools, such as Regent's Park Community Primary School, Birmingham (DfES 2003a). The school has developed a programme of support for promoting the use of pupils' first language with the aim of raising academic achievement. Strategies include:

- A recruitment policy to appoint staff with relevant bilingual skills.

- The provision of appropriate resources which celebrate linguistic and cultural diversity.

- Lunchtime language clubs where older pupils support younger pupils.

- The encouragement of parents to work in the classroom and develop tapes and story sacks in the home languages.

Another helpful book on this theme (reviewed later in Chapter 3) is *Enriching Literacy – Text, Talk and Tales in Today's Classroom*, produced by Brent Language Service (1999). Case studies are given, together with some practical strategies for supporting both English language and home language development. Emphasis is placed on the need for cognitively challenging activities and suggestions are given as to how this can be achieved, for example:

- Effective questioning (*Taxonomy of Educational Objectives Bloom* 1956).

- Scaffolding (Vygotsky 1962; Hammond 2001).

- Collaborative group work – problem-solving activities.

Implications for Practice

- Recognition of the knowledge, culture and language which bilingual pupils bring to learning.

- Focused support to secure full access to the curriculum.

- Commitment to partnership approaches in the deployment of additional resources.

- Reflection on teaching and learning strategies.

Whilst additional adults in the classroom bring a range of expertise to the support of new arrivals, it is clear that the established routines of the National Literacy and National Numeracy Strategies (now the Primary National Strategy) are very important in supporting the needs of pupils from diverse backgrounds. Whole-class modelling and teacher demonstration of English as well as mathematical routines are important. Guided and supported activities are also useful in securing the learning of these pupils. Teaching assistants can have an important supporting role in this area. Strategies to support include:

- Explaining instructions, tasks and curriculum content.

- Redefining words and phrases critical to a child's understanding.

- Encouraging children to articulate ideas in their preferred language.

- Developing children's confidence in expressing themselves in English.

- Presenting themselves (as workers) as role models.

- Promoting home–school liaison.

How many of these are part of your practice?

Likewise in both English and mathematics, a child's first language should form part of the teaching and learning experience wherever possible. Not only does it aid the development of new concepts, which transfer to the second language, but it also has a positive impact on children's self-concept and self-esteem.

Activity Sheet – Classroom Observation and Self-Assessment

Enrol the help of a colleague to observe your teaching and note how many of these strategies you use in your classroom practice.

Keep a record of your own practices over the period of a week and ask your colleague to give you feedback on their observations of your use of the strategies.

Remember most professionals learn a lot through the professional conversations they have with colleagues.

There are bound to be areas in which you can develop your practice.

Academic attainment

In the DfES report *Aiming High: Raising the Achievement of Minority Ethnic Pupils* (DfES 2003a), it states that new data from the Pupil Level Annual School Census (PLASC) in 2002 confirmed that pupils of Chinese and Indian heritage achieve above average results but that Black pupils and pupils of Pakistani and Bangladeshi heritage are under-achieving.

The report also highlights some of the factors that contribute to under-achievement including low teacher expectations, the length of settlement and period of schooling in the UK and fluency in English. It states that where parents have a high level of education and/or have high aspirations for their children then these can be strong factors in achievement among pupils.

Strategies	Your own use of these strategies	How could you improve?
Explaining instructions, tasks, curriculum content and rephrasing words critical to a child's understanding		
Using cognitively challenging activities, e.g. collaborative group work/problem solving		
Encouraging children to articulate ideas in their preferred language		
Developing children's confidence in expressing themselves in English		
Presenting themselves (as workers) as role models		
Promoting home–school liaison		

Common issues in attainment

Below are some of the common issues concerning the raising of attainment in schools. Five key areas are identified in the DfES report as characteristics of schools that successfully raise the achievement of minority ethnic pupils:

■ strong leadership – the headteacher and senior teachers lead an effective strategy that is applied across the whole school;

■ effective teaching and learning;

■ high expectations – these expectations are underpinned by the practical use of data and monitoring. Policies and examination results are monitored for their effect on particular groups of pupils to pinpoint and tackle under-performance;

■ an ethos of respect with a clear approach to racism and bad behaviour;

■ parental involvement – parents and the wider community are positively encouraged to play a full part in the life and development of the school.

What does the evidence look like in your school?

(The theme of raising academic attainment runs throughout the book, and we explore this with particular reference to bilingual learners in Chapter 3, 'Black boys' in Chapter 4, and UK Gypsy, Roma and Traveller children in Chapter 5.)

Checklist for an induction programme

From the discussion so far a number of themes have emerged as to how new arrivals should be helped to settle in and begin to achieve academically. Here we draw together the main points of the discussion to provide an outline for an induction programme, signalling a list of things that schools and practitioners can do to enhance this process. An induction policy should not be seen in isolation, but in the context of existing and complementary school policies. For example, Section 71(1) of the Race Relations Amendment Act places a general duty on schools to eliminate unlawful racial discrimination and to promote equality of opportunity and good relations between people of different racial groups (CRE 2000). As a result schools have implemented policy on racial harassment and equal opportunities. Other school policies relevant to the question of induction are those concerning bullying and school behaviour.

With the wider school context in mind, the following induction model highlights what practitioners should do when a new pupil arrives. This is informed by a model produced by Derby City Access Service, but all local authorities are obliged to implement policy along these lines whereby practitioners:

■ Provide a friendly, supportive environment – ensure that all staff are aware of the school's ethos for children, and those with English as an additional language.

■ Make staff aware of the school's equal opportunities and anti-racism policy.

- Use an Initial Assessment of New Arrivals Form to profile the new pupil – these forms are normally provided by the school and/or the local authority.

- Inform the Access Service or equivalent unit in the local authority – they may be able to offer assistance.

- Establish which language(s) the child or young person uses, any experience they may have of the English language, which countries they have lived in and whether anyone at home speaks English.

- Place the child/young person in an appropriate friendship group.

- Devote adequate time for the new pupil to become familiar with the school layout, and as much as possible, the school rules.

- Make the pupil and family aware of the home–school agreement – the DfEE booklet *Home–School Agreements* is available in Bengali, Chinese, Gujarati, Hindi, Punjabi and Urdu.

- Find out if any member of staff speaks the child's language or try to identify a community representative – they may be able to assist with the initial assessment and settling-in period.

(Adapted from a leaflet produced by Derby City Access Service 1999.)

In addition there are some general issues to note about the settling-in process. Newly arrived children learning English as an additional language may have high cognitive ability but initially they may begin with a 'silent period', and 'culture shock' may cause a delay in obvious signs of understanding (Cummins 1996). This is part of the cross-cultural learning experience. Children may be used to teachers of one gender only, or being educated within half-day sessions. They may feel tiredness caused by operating in a new language environment, or as we noted earlier, experience trauma attached to the circumstances which caused them to leave their original home (Richman 1998; Rutter 2001). They may also find the experience of attending school a novel but anxious activity. For example, newly arrived Czech and Polish pupils from Romany backgrounds may have experienced victimization whilst attending school and from society in general (Sinfin Community School 2003). Pupils may also be taking classes in their own language at supplementary schools, which involves attending evening or weekend classes or may be maintaining their home language through correspondence courses.

To assist in the demanding process of adapting to a new educational experience, beneficial classroom practice should include:

- Legible handwriting – on the board and in handouts.

- A helpful layout of information.

- Careful use of the voice – with clear diction and sufficient volume.

- Visual aids – to support meaning.

- Clear physical indications – touching or lifting up a piece of equipment, pointing closely to a section of text and so on.

- Saying the pupil's name – to gain their attention, and to ensure from the beginning that you can pronounce it properly.

- Use of simple but grammatical English – not 'pidgin English'.

- Short, clear explanations where possible.

- The breaking up of a long talk into stages lasting a few minutes each.

- Summarizing at the beginning and end of a long talk, and recapping at various stages throughout.

- The use of bilingual dictionaries.

(Adapted from a leaflet produced by Derby City Access Service 1999)

It is also important to consider 'survival language' – the basic words and phrases that a new pupil needs in order to survive the first few weeks in a strange environment, for example:

Hello

Goodbye

Please may I have ………….

Where is …………………….?

I don't understand

Thank you …………….……

We will return to some of the points concerning language acquisition and anti-racist practice later in the book but here we summarize the key points of this chapter.

Key Points

- Diversity is changing in the classroom.

- Induction procedures for new arrivals are essential.

- Working with a multi-agency approach will contribute to a successful induction process and the on-going educational experience of pupils.

- Recognizing and valuing the home languages of all children is important as these have a positive impact on their cognitive development.

- Teachers need to reflect on their own practice and include cognitively challenging activities to raise the academic attainment of all children.

- The most effective schools are those which have a whole-school approach to these issues and have developed partnerships between home, school and local community.

▶

■ An induction procedure should incorporate the time and opportunity to both assess and welcome new arrivals into the school with a recognition that many pupils develop in stages, one of which may be a 'silent period' whilst the new environment and language are being absorbed.

We look next in Chapter 3 at one particular group highlighted in this discussion – those pupils who speak English as an additional language.

Supporting EAL pupils

This chapter looks at:

■ the ethos of the school and classroom

■ recognizing and valuing home languages

■ assessment for learning

■ planning and teaching.

This chapter has been written for teachers and teaching assistants with little or no experience of teaching new arrivals. It can be daunting to find oneself in an unfamiliar situation and very frustrating for both teacher and pupil when neither understands each other! 'How do I begin?' is a question that is frequently asked and this chapter is an attempt to try and answer that question using practical suggestions. Some anecdotes are used to illustrate a few of the difficulties that can arise when supporting bilingual pupils. They are all taken from our own personal experience and they have been selected to illustrate some of the difficulties facing non-specialist teachers of EAL pupils. Four areas will be highlighted, beginning with a discussion about the ethos of the school and classroom.

The ethos of the school and classroom

Rutter argues 'A good induction policy is particularly important for refugee students ... It aims to make the first crucial weeks in a new school a happy experience' (2001: 95). The question is what constitutes a good induction policy? Read the following case study. The headteacher thought that he had put good practice into place but the following incident illustrates how difficult it is to translate policy into effective practice.

Case Study

The headteacher showed two Turkish girls and their mother around the school. There was an interpreter present and all information about the school was translated for them. The girls were shown their classrooms and met their new teachers. The following day they arrived smiling and keen to start. However, later that day one of the girls wanted to go to

▶

the toilet but had forgotten how to ask to go to the toilet in English. She wet herself and became very upset. She would not let anyone help her. The class teacher suggested that the girl's mother should be contacted. Unfortunately when the headteacher contacted her he forgot that she did not speak English. There was frustration and upset on all sides.

Activity – Supporting the individual pupil

Imagine that you are that class teacher.

What strategies would you use to help this new pupil from Turkey to be able to ask to go to the toilet?

It has been suggested that being able to ask to go to the toilet is not important in the grand world of academia and the labyrinth of the National Curriculum. However we would argue strongly that this is one of the most useful words that a new arrival will need, particularly at primary school level. To avoid an embarrassing situation such as the one described above, one solution to the toilet problem might be to give the pupil a series of little picture cards on a key-ring on admission. One picture could be a toilet. In this way the pupil can show the picture card to the teacher and is not forced into speaking English until he or she is ready. It is vital that the new arrival feels safe and secure and that everything is done to lessen what is a very stressful and alien situation. Another strategy is for the class teacher to learn the word for toilet or to ask the parent how to pronounce the word for toilet in the home language. For older pupils a bilingual dictionary is helpful.

In this case study the headteacher had a good admissions and induction procedure. He had tried to ensure a smooth transition for the girls but even the best laid plans can sometimes go wrong. That wet Tuesday morning was a steep learning curve for all concerned and the headteacher and the class teacher both had to realize that induction and admission procedures require more than just a tour of the school.

The two girls did make good progress and the elder girl felt confident enough to take part in the school's end-of-term production. She stood confidently on the stage after only one term and sang songs with the rest of her class!

According to the DfES document (2004a) *Aiming High: Supporting the Effective Use of EMAG*, 9.7 per cent of all pupils in schools are recorded as EAL and this reflects a growing bilingual population. It is as a result of this growing population that teachers and teaching assistants need INSET (In-Service Training) and guidance in supporting these pupils. It is the intention of this chapter to provide some concrete examples of how to support EAL pupils and to explore some of the surrounding issues.

Time to reflect

Imagine that you have been whisked away to another country.

Would you have the confidence to ask where the toilet is, using the language of that country?

In how many different languages can you say the word 'toilet'?

(There are some suggestions at the end of the chapter!)

The *ethos* of the school and the classroom is very important. It is vital to give newly arrived pupils the time and space to settle in and adapt to their new surroundings. This is necessary for all children but even more so for those children who do not speak English. One effective strategy is to provide a 'buddy' for the new pupil. A 'buddy' is someone, usually a pupil in the same class, who will sit with them, play with them and generally look after them. However, it is important to acknowledge the role of the 'buddy' and Bolloten and Spafford (2003) suggest a Certificate of Merit could be awarded to the 'buddy' during an assembly, in recognition of the time and help given.

First impressions count and as that new pupil enters the school gates with his or her parents they will begin to notice the school environment. Some schools have 'Welcome' written in many different languages and displays with labels that reflect the languages of the school. Helping to create a warm, inviting environment both within the classroom and within the whole school is very important. The following audit is one way of reflecting on the ethos of your own school and classroom:

Activities – Is your school environment welcoming?

- Is there a 'Welcome' poster in different languages on your main entrance door?
- Are there labels in different languages on your displays?
- Do your displays reflect different cultures?
- Are there any dual-language books in your library and classroom?
- Is there a buddy system in place?
- Do you have 'Buddy Certificates' or special assemblies?

Maslow (1954) highlighted a 'Hierarchy of Needs' which we all need in order to achieve our full potential. He displayed his ideas in the form of a pyramid. It is important to note the first level of physiological needs and how this relates to some of our more vulnerable children.

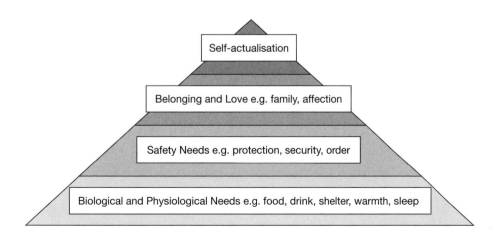

Case Study

Some of the more vulnerable children in our schools are asylum seeker and refugee pupils. As teachers we are not always aware of what they may have experienced on their journey to this country. One Nursery teacher described how each day food was put out on the table for children to eat as part of their snack routine. She was surprised that food kept 'disappearing' and she was not sure what was happening. The teacher decided to carry out an observation and she noticed that one of the newly arrived pupils from Somalia was taking food and hiding it around the nursery. She discovered by talking to the little boy's mother that for them food had been scarce and they had had to look for food on the journey and then hide it in order to survive. The little boy was encouraged to eat during snack time with the other children and to ask for more if he was still hungry. In order to help pupils to move towards achieving their full potential it is vital that the basic needs of the pupils are accommodated.

For many of us it is difficult to imagine some of the hardships that our pupils have encountered and because it takes time to adjust, pupils and parents may not want to talk about their experiences. All too often we as practitioners become engrossed in the lessons that we have planned and we sometimes fail to notice the signs and behaviours that indicate that the biological and physiological needs, as Maslow described, are not being met. Until we begin to address these basic needs then effective language learning will not take place.

Some pupils may have experienced sleep deprivation and some may have witnessed distressing scenes. Consequently they may not be feeling safe either in their new country or at home, or even within the school environment. The second level of Maslow's 'Hierarchy of Needs' refers to the 'Safety Needs' of children. It is essential to try and ensure that children feel safe and secure when they are in the school environment. The following case study illustrates how a sudden noise triggered a negative reaction in a child who had recently arrived from Kosovo. It is not possible to cover every eventuality, but as professionals we do need to prepare ourselves and understand what some of these families have experienced so that we can support them more effectively. It is important to be aware of some of the conflicts that are happening around the world.

Case Study

A teacher was taking her class swimming one day and they were walking across the playground towards the bus that would take them to the swimming pool. Suddenly a can of deodorant fell from one of the pupil's bags and crashed onto the playground. One of the boys threw himself down onto the playground floor and covered his head with his hands. He was extremely distressed and unnerved by what had happened. The pupil was from Kosovo and he had witnessed violence at first-hand. The noise of the can falling onto the playground caused a flash-back and his immediate reaction was to fall down and protect himself from the perceived danger.

Activities – The emotional well-being of pupils

- What do you know about the emotional well-being of your asylum seeker/refugee pupils/EU Accession State pupils?

- Have you noticed any behaviours that may indicate that one of your pupils is feeling insecure and unsafe?

- Imagine that you are taking your class swimming and one of your pupils becomes distressed because a loud noise is heard. He or she is clearly frightened by the noise. What can you do to help this child feel safe and secure?

The Refugee Council provides training and there are many different courses including 'The Emotional Wellbeing of Asylum and Refugee Pupils'.

It is important to remember that younger children may display some of their fears and anxieties in their play and they need to be reassured. They also need to be allowed to express these feelings in a creative way. Wilkes states that 'It is very difficult for these children to deal with the emotional horrors they have experienced … Many find it hard to put how they feel into words and are reluctant to discuss their experiences' (1994: 9).

Case Study

One young French-speaking girl from the Congo was playing in the role play area one afternoon. She appeared to be quite content on her own. We observed her make a gun shape with her hands. She then made shooting noises and pointed at the floor saying 'Il est mort! Il est mort!' (He's dead! He's dead!).

This pupil was enacting something that she had possibly witnessed and was incorporating it into her play. She was not distressed at that moment in time but other pupils can be very distressed and some may display aggressive behaviours. Trying to find creative ways to help with the emotional well-being of new arrivals can be very challenging!

Activities – Using creativity

What would you do to help a child to explore their feelings?

Art and design, drama and music are all creative ways of helping vulnerable pupils, especially asylum seeker and refugee pupils, to express themselves.

Inviting musicians and theatre groups from local communities to perform is another way of helping pupils raise their esteem

Herbert (2003) of the Refugee Achievement Project in Westminster has produced a programme of work which is intended for use with the whole class in PSHE and Citizenship for Key Stages 1 and 2. There are photocopiable activity sheets and the report states that 'The topic lends itself particularly well to drama, music and other creative activities. During the course of the programme, children with a refugee background may feel able to share their own or their family's experiences *but should never be made to feel obligated to do so*' (2003: 3). (authors' emphasis)

One activity suggests finding different 'welcome' words in other languages.

Activities – Words of welcome!

How many different words of greeting can you say?

	Greeting Word	Language
1		
2		
3		

It can be reassuring and often a source of some amusement when pupils hear their teacher attempting to use a different language. It is a first step in establishing a rapport and in building bridges between cultures.

The use of a first or home language will now be explored in this next section.

Recognizing and valuing the home language

> No child should be expected to cast off the language and culture of the home as he crosses the school threshold, nor to live and act as though school and home represent two totally separate and different cultures which have to be kept firmly apart (Bullock Report, DES 1975: 286).

This well-known quotation serves to illustrate the fact that the issue of valuing first/home languages is not a new one. It is an area that has been researched and debated for decades (see the Rampton (1981), Swann (DES 1985) and MacPherson (1999) Reports).

In a video that accompanies the National Literacy Strategy (DfES, 1998a) materials, there is an interview with a teacher called Maria who recalls how she felt when she first came to this country and was told *not* to speak her own language. She felt embarrassed if her parents spoke to her in Greek and her brother was given an English-sounding name because the teacher was unable to pronounce her brother's Greek name. Her first/home language was not valued and her bilingualism was seen as a problem and not something to be celebrated (Blackledge 2000, Smyth 2002).

One of the exemplary case studies on the DfES Standards website highlights the outstanding work of Regent's Park Primary School in Birmingham. The school is a multi-ethnic and multilingual inner city primary school in an area of high unemployment and social deprivation. In

2001 it was recognised by OFSTED as a successful school and gained beacon status. The DfES website states 'The head teacher, senior staff and members of the then Section 11-funded EAL team were committed to the promotion and development of the children's first languages'.

They had wanted to promote first languages in order to celebrate the different languages and cultures of the school because they believed that this helped to raise self-esteem and build confidence. They also believed that it would support children by helping them to learn new concepts through the use of their home or first language.

The success of Regent's Park did not happen overnight. Bilingual staff were employed who reflected the culture of the pupils. INSET was delivered on developing the use of a first or home language.

A *whole-school policy* was produced and children were encouraged to use their first/home language skills throughout all areas of the curriculum. One successful initiative was to promote peer group support and to encourage 'paired talk' or 'talking partners' in the first or home language.

The report states 'Pupils who shared a language even though they may have had different degrees of proficiency, were paired together to encourage the development and use of first language to clarify understanding'.

The headteacher's vision was of 'talking classrooms where bilingualism is celebrated and used to extend pupils' skills' and the recognition that speaking English as an additional language is not a barrier to learning but of positive benefit. An investigation that the headteacher had carried out revealed the following:

- Teachers/adults did most of the talking.

- Pupils did the least.

- There was a lack of understanding of group work.

- Pupils supported by bilingual adults were in awe of them or were being translated to.

It was as a result of this that she vowed to change these practices and to create a school environment that promoted pupil talk and the use of a home language.

Time to reflect

How many languages are spoken in your school?

How many different languages are spoken in your classroom?

Do you promote the use of first/home languages?

Who talks most in your classroom?

Research by Cummins (1996) helps us to understand some of the benefits of bilingual education and the advantages of being bilingual. Cummins maintains that there are cognitive benefits such as the transference of reading and writing skills from one language to another.

There are also personal benefits that can raise self-esteem and the benefit to other children because they begin to develop an understanding of other languages and cultures which in turn helps to promote cultural diversity. Cummins notes:

> In general, it is not surprising that bilingual children should be more adept at certain aspects of linguistic processing. In gaining control over two language systems, the bilingual child has had to decipher much more language input than the monolingual child who has been exposed to only one language system. Thus, the bilingual child has had considerably more practice in analyzing meaning than the monolingual child. (1996: 167)

Case Study

A teacher at an inner-city primary school realized that in the Literacy Hour there seemed to be a shortage of 'Big Books' that reflected the language and culture of her pupils. She decided to write her own story and to translate it into Urdu. Both pupils and parents were involved in this exciting project and the story illustrated an important event for Muslim families – the *Hajj*. When the story was read in both English and in Urdu the children became very excited and wanted to share with their teacher their own experiences. The teacher was encouraged to develop this strategy and to promote bilingual 'Big Books' as part of the Literacy Hour.

Activities – Test your knowledge!

■ What does the word *Hajj* mean?

■ Why is it important to Muslims?

(Answers at the end of the chapter!)

There are implications here in terms of classroom practice. It is important to acknowledge the languages and cultures of the pupils in our classrooms and to encourage the use of home languages. However, good practice can only take place if it is embedded within a whole-school vision. A language policy needs to be developed and incorporated into school development plans. This view is stressed in the DfES document *Aiming High: Guidance on Supporting the Education of Asylum Seeking and Refugee Children* (2004b). It states 'Developing a language policy in a setting is crucial to meeting the needs of children' (p. 6).

The document maintains that good practice should include professional development for all staff, the purchase of suitable resources and the development of home–school partnerships. It makes reference to the importance of finding out about the languages of the school and to make every effort to at least be able to greet pupils in their own language.

Having admitted new arrivals to your school and created a welcoming environment it is then time to assess the pupil concerned in order to help you to plan and teach more effectively.

Assessment for learning

Edwards (1998: 24) noted that 'The assessment of second language learners is extremely problematic'. Nevertheless, it can be argued that it is important to carry out an initial language assessment when pupils arrive in order to create a language baseline from which progress in English language development can be measured. In some schools there are often bilingual staff who can assess pupils in their home language and this helps to build up a picture of what pupils already know. However, with the arrival and dispersal of asylum seeker and refugee families and pupils from EU Accession states there are many different languages now spoken in our schools but there are not always staff in schools who can speak all the different languages represented. According to the QCA document *A Language in Common* (2000), about 200 different languages are currently used throughout England.

Prior to the publication of this document, EAL pupils were assessed as 'W' or working towards Level 1 of the National Curriculum. It was possible for a pupil to enter the Reception class and be assessed as 'W' in Speaking and at the end of Key Stage 1 to still be assessed as 'W' if he or she has not achieved Level 1 of the National Curriculum. The teacher would know whether that pupil had made progress, but this was not reflected in the grading system.

In addition to this some local authorities used an assessment system based on Hilary Hester's 'Stages' and there was wide variation in the use of these scales (Hester et al. 1993).

In order to have a consistent approach to assessing EAL pupils the government produced the document *A Language in Common* (QCA 2000) to help teachers to assess more accurately those pupils operating below Level 1 of the National Curriculum. (This assessment is sometimes known as the 'QCA Steps' assessment.)

Activities – Identifying language targets

Imagine that you are a Year 5 teacher and a Polish pupil has recently joined your class. Read the following case study and language assessment.

What language targets would you need to set?.

Case Study

Language Assessment (Year 5 – Polish speaker)

S. can give his name and age upon request.

He is able to name nine colours accurately in English. He is unsure of purple and grey.

S. can name some parts of the body including head, hair, nose, eyes and mouth. He is unsure of shoulders, arms and feet. He was not able to name any transport vocabulary except for the picture of the big car and he said,

'Limousine!'

S. can write his name but he does not know the names of the letters of the alphabet. However he does know 22 corresponding sounds. He was unsure of h, i, x and y.

▶

S. can count from 1–20 in English and, with support, in tens from 10–100.

He was encouraged to look at a dual-language storybook. The story was *The Enormous Turnip* and it was written in both English and Polish. S. was very happy to be able to read it in Polish. He was encouraged to look at the pictures. He was not able to retell the story or talk about the pictures in Polish. He pointed to single objects and named some items of vocabulary. He was asked some simple comprehension questions about the picture but he was unable to reply in English.

S. is beginning to echo expressions that he hears and is beginning to use single words. He responds to greetings and can answer simple questions about himself. He is operating at QCA Step 1 in his Listening and Speaking.

The reality for many teachers today is exactly this – that they can find themselves in situations such as the one described above. How does one plan for a Year 5 Polish pupil whose spoken level of English is below Level 1 of the National Curriculum? How can he be included in the Literacy Hour?

The pupil in the case study was assessed at QCA Level Step 1 and his speech sample revealed that he was beginning to name objects and that he was using mainly single words. Collecting speech or oral samples is one way of collating evidence of language development and progression in the new target language and this then helps in the identification of language targets.

It states in the Primary National Strategy materials, *Excellence and Enjoyment: Learning and Teaching for Bilingual Children in the Primary Years* (DfES 2006d) that

> the use of work samples, oral language samples and question-level analysis drawn from across the curriculum to identify strengths and areas for development in children's responses enables the identification of areas of the curriculum which pose particular challenges to bilingual learners and the language learning required to access these aspects of the curriculum (Unit 1, p. 31).

Once a language assessment has been carried out then language targets can be set and planning and teaching can begin.

The next section of this chapter examines some practical strategies for supporting EAL pupils and helping them to access the mainstream curriculum.

Planning and teaching

Gibbons (2002) argues that there are two sets of information that form the basis for planning which integrate second language learning and curriculum learning. She suggests that the following two questions should be posed:

- What are the language demands of the curriculum?
- What do children currently know about language and what are their language-learning needs?

Gibbons maintains that although teachers are very familiar with planning and thinking about curricular aims, many are not so accustomed to thinking about language aims and objectives and in particular the language needs of their EAL pupils.

Language aims and objectives

What spoken language demands will there be?

What listening tasks will there be?

What texts will students be reading?

What are the written text types that will occur?

What aspects of grammar (e.g. tense) does the topic require students to use?

What specific vocabulary does the topic require students to know?

The following activity is taken from Gibbons (op.cit) and is a useful aid in planning:

The Renewed Framework for literacy and mathematics provides a concise overview to planning for language development. It states that planning for EAL learners is most effective when:

- It is part of the planning process of the whole school and the whole class and is embedded in the usual planning format.

- It takes account of the language demands of the curriculum, both subject-specific vocabulary and the appropriate language forms associated with content.

- It provides opportunities for speaking and listening, collaborative work and other strategies for language development.

(Taken from *Excellence and Enjoyment: Planning and Assessment for Learning*, DfES 2006d)

Also, it is important to plan for any additional adults who may be supporting in your classroom. If there is a language support teacher or teaching assistant, it is vital that they are involved in the planning process and that they know what the language aim of a lesson is and what key vocabulary needs to be taught or even pre-taught. In order to help access the Literacy Hour, it has been found that for some first-stage language learners it can be helpful for a parent or bilingual assistant to read the 'Big Book' in the home language prior to the first lesson and

Time to reflect! – Improving the opportunities for speaking and listening

Are there many opportunities in your planning for speaking and listening activities?

Do you include a language aim for your EAL pupils?

Consider how you would include key vocabulary that is needed to access any given lesson.

for some of the key vocabulary to be discussed and explained. In this way EAL pupils will have some idea of what they are listening to during the session.

In order to help teachers empathize with this situation the DfES (2002) in their training materials have produced a video of a 'Gujerati Literacy Hour'. For those of us unable to speak or to understand Gujerati it is difficult to access the story that is being read and when this video extract has been used in training sessions teachers have described their own feelings of inadequacy. They mention how quickly they 'switch off' from what is happening. Others search in vain for some clue as to what the story is about. It helps us to remember that for some EAL pupils this is what it may be like for them sitting and listening to the Literacy Hour in our classrooms.

Activities – Making sense of a different language

Imagine that you have been transported to a school in a different country and you do not speak that language. You are listening to a story being read and you do not understand what is being said.

What would help you to make sense of what you are hearing and seeing?

List three ideas that would help you to understand better:

Your ideas will help you to use appropriate strategies with your EAL pupils.

Some key strategies for helping EAL pupils to access the curriculum are described in the book *Enriching Literacy – text, talk and tales in today's classroom* (Brent 1999). It states that 'The route for bilingual learners from everyday English to curriculum English needs to go via classroom activities which make much use of key visuals, collaborative group work and writing frames … ' (p. 24).

Key visuals may include pictures, photographs, maps, drawings, graphs, grids and charts. However, it is how they are used that is important. The story of *Grandpa's Handkerchief* by Dorothy Clark is illustrated in grid form as an example of how this could be used to illustrate the story (Brent 1999: 32).

Day of the Week	Colour	Use
Monday	Blue	To wipe away a crumb
Thursday	Red	To make a sun hat
Wednesday	Green	To cheer the team
Tuesday	Pink	To remind him about a birthday
Sunday	Orange	To play pirates
Saturday	White	To wave at a train
Friday	Yellow	To bandage a knee

This type of key visual is a form of scaffolding and is used to help pupils to sequence the story and to aid their comprehension. It could be introduced as a paired activity and used to rehearse the language orally to start with and then used as a writing frame. The language structure of 'On Monday' can be rehearsed with the other days of the week in a meaningful context. A grid such as this can involve all four language elements – listening, speaking, reading and writing.

Activities – Making the Literacy Hour accessible to EAL pupils

Think about the next book that you are going to use in the Literacy Hour.

What key visuals could you develop and use to make it more accessible to the EAL pupils in your class?

What language would you need to model?

Have you ever used scaffolding as a strategy? Consider its use in your present teaching.

Modelling the language and scaffolding the language are two important strategies. Using repetitive texts and customizing texts are also helpful strategies. Moreover, some teachers have found the activities used in the intervention programme 'Talking Partners' to be very effective. 'Talking Partners' is a ten-week speaking and listening intervention programme that was developed by colleagues in Bradford and it aims to accelerate language learning in children. It consists of three 20 minute sessions a week and the recommended ratio is one adult to three pupils (Kotler et al. 2002).

There are six different activities including news telling, retelling familiar and unfamiliar stories, character studies, barrier games and reporting back. All of these are directly related to the Literacy Hour. The ability to retell a story or to use the language of instruction in barrier games is an essential component of literacy work. If pupils can manage these tasks orally then gradually these skills will transfer into their written work and the task of writing a story or a list of instructions will not be so daunting to them.

However, how do we know that any of these strategies are successful? A small-scale pilot project (Sanders in Richardson and Wood 2004) was carried out in a Derby City primary school to ascertain how effective the 'Talking Partners' intervention programme was. The pilot project was targeted at pupils of Pakistani origin as a response to raising the achievement of minority ethnic pupils and in particular with under-achieving groups of pupils. (We also look at works within the RAISE Project in Chapter 4.) The pupils were all at Key Stage 1 and were Mirpuri–Punjabi speakers. Their spoken skills were tested before the start of the intervention programme and again after it. The pre-test results showed that there was as much as two years difference between the test age and the chronological age (for some pupils they are operating at two years below their actual age in terms of semantic development, and for one pupil in the pilot two years and eight months behind in his syntactical development). After the ten-week intervention programme was completed the same test was administered again and the results were analysed. These showed that there was an average gain of 14.5 months in terms of vocabulary acquisition and an average gain of 12.8 months in terms of grammar development.

One of the conclusions of this small-scale study was:

All specialist teachers of English as an additional language would benefit from Talking Partners training, as would all teaching assistants who have occasion to work with children developing as bilingual learners. (p. 68)

Talking Partners draws attention to the links between oracy and literacy and focuses on the development of Cognitive Academic Language Proficiency (CALP).

Activities – Useful readings

Do you understand the difference between Basic Interpersonal Communicative Skills (BICS) and Cognitive Academic Language Proficiency (CALP)?

Further reading on this can be found in *Supporting Bilingual Learners In Schools* by Gravelle 2000 (Chapter 2: 21) and in Cummins 2003 (Chapter 3: 64).

A glossary of teaching activities is provided in Gibbons (2002) and Gravelle (2000) summarizes some of these ideas thus: 'Bilingual learners will be successful in a classroom with a positive and supportive ethos in which talk has a central place. Collaborative activities can provide the ideal context for such exploratory talk' (p. 165).

There are no quick-fix solutions to supporting EAL pupils. However, an attempt has been made in this chapter to highlight four areas where significant differences can be made. The list is not exhaustive. Stop now and reflect on what you have read and think about some of the areas that you would like to discover more about. Remember that what is good practice for EAL pupils is good practice for all!

Time to reflect – Unlocking the door!

From each of the four sections choose four ideas that you would like to find out more about to help you to support your EAL pupils more effectively:

◆ Ethos of the school and classroom

◆ Valuing the importance of home languages

◆ Assessment for learning

◆ Planning and teaching

Answers to the *Hajj* activity

What does *Hajj* mean?

Hajj is a pilgrimage to Mecca which brings together Muslims of all races from all over the world.

Why is it important to Muslims?

It is important for Muslims because in carrying out this obligation they fulfil one of the five 'pillars' of Islam.

How many different words for 'toilet' did you find?

Here are some translations for the word 'toilet':

Albanian – *toilet*

Somali – *musqul*

Portuguese – *sanita*

Polish – *muszla klozetowa*

Turkish – *Tuvalet*

Key Points

- Effective practice for supporting EAL pupils can be divided into four areas including the ethos of the school and the classroom, recognizing and valuing home languages, assessment for learning and planning and teaching.

- The difference between basic, social or 'playground' English and academic or classroom English needs to be recognized and planned for accordingly.

We look next at strategies for raising the attainment of 'Black boys'.

CHAPTER 4

Raising 'Black Boys'' attainment

> This chapter looks at:
>
> ■ understanding the context
>
> ■ social class
>
> ■ gender
>
> ■ ethnicity
>
> ■ mentoring
>
> ■ the inclusive curriculum
>
> ■ intervention programmes
>
> ■ British Pakistani and Bangladeshi learners.

All pupils should ... identify and respect the differences and similarities between people (*The National Curriculum*, QCA1999).

In this chapter we explore the issue of under-achievement among Black and minority ethnic boys and highlight strategies to help raise attainment.

Understanding the context

Under-achievement among ethnic groups in the UK is not new – as we noted earlier in Chapter 1, concern has been expressed for several decades (Coard 1971). However, recent government reports about the academic performance of Black and minority ethnic (bme) boys places the issue high on the educational agenda as this group of learners are attaining below the national average, and they also form 'a high exclusion group' (Blair 2001; DfES 2003a; Mouchel Parkman Report 2003). A lack of educational qualifications can and does lead to social exclusion, and their absence in the labour market leads to failure in achieving full potential.

In terms of the teaching profession, 'Qualifying to Teach' (TTA 2002) which was highlighted in Chapter 1, recognizes the need to reinforce expectations of awareness, skills and knowledge for trainee teachers in respect of the teaching of those pupils who speak English as an additional language, and others from diverse backgrounds. At the same time, government reports have emphasized the need to develop appropriate strategies to raise the academic attainment of all pupils. For example, a study for OFSTED in 1996 by Gillborn and Gripps concluded that if ethnic diversity is ignored and differences in educational achievement are not examined, considerable injustices are sanctioned and enormous potential is wasted (OFSTED 1996a). Within this, specific learners have been identified:

> Black Caribbean pupils, despite notable exceptions, were … generally underrepresented in the higher levels of both Key Stages 1 and 2. (OFSTED 1996a:11)

Crucially, evidence suggests that 'Black boys' start their schooling at broadly the same level as other pupils, but in the course of their studies they fall further and further behind. If we broaden this out to include 'Black African', we find:

> in national examinations African Caribbean boys have been the lowest achieving group at practically every key stage for the last four years. (LDA 2004)

African pupils have generally attained more highly than African Caribbean pupils, but they are still at the lower end of the achievement spectrum (ibid).

More recently, there has been documented evidence of improvement among some 'Black boys' which suggests that the government initiatives to tackle under-achievement in this group, particularly since 2003, may be having an effect. For example, official statistics show that the GCSE exam results of Black pupils have increased over the last two years above the national average, and the group that improved most was that of Black Caribbean learners.

The percentage of pupils achieving five or more A* to C grades at GCSE in 2005 were as follows:

- White – up 2.8 percentage points to 55.1 per cent

- Black Carribean – up 6 percentage points to 41.7 per cent

- Black African – up 5 percentages points to 48.3 per cent

- Pakistani – up 3.2 percentage points to 48.4 per cent

- Bangladeshi – up 4.3 percentage points to 52.7 per cent

- All pupils in maintained schools: up 3 percentage points.

(www.dfes.gov.uk/rsgateway)

Whilst there is, therefore, some evidence of improvement, it is still important to sustain efforts to support this group of learners.

Significantly, the two groups which perform considerably below the national average for all Key Stages and at GCSE are Gypsy, Roma and Traveller pupils (except at Key Stage 2), and pupils who are eligible for free school meals. (The latter group is outside the remit of this book, but raising the attainment of Gypsy, Roma and Traveller children in the UK forms the basis of the discussion in the next chapter.)

The work of Gillborn and Gipps (OFSTED 1996a) and Gillborn and Mirza (2000) has made clear the differences among minority ethnic groups and the fact that not all minority ethnic groups fail to attain. For example, their review of literature in the field concluded that Indian pupils were the highest performing South Asian group and that in some localities they were achieving in excess of their White counterparts. This was confirmed by Demack et al:

> the attainment of Indian pupils suggests that English as an Additional Language is not an impenetrable barrier to achievement. (2000: 10)

Gillborn and Mirza (2000) also highlight the difference in achievement among different authorities for these minority ethnic pupils:

> Although at the national level Pakistani youth are less likely to attain five higher grade GCSEs than their white peers, this pattern is reversed in some areas. In four out of ten LAs that monitor by ethnic progress Pakistani pupils are more likely to attain this bench-mark than white pupils locally. (2000: 10)

Similarly, in the London borough of Tower Hamlets, where approximately 25 per cent of the country's Bangladeshi children are educated, pupils are attaining higher average exam scores than their White counterparts (Gillborn and Mirza 2000). The pattern of under-achievement is, therefore, a 'fragmented pattern': there is no clear picture of achievement within minority ethnic groups and we need to be cautious about applying generalizations about 'Asians' and African Caribbean groups of learners (Gaine 2005). Where there is evidence of achievement, however, we should ask what is taking place in some authorities and in some schools which allows this to happen and what lessons can be learnt by others practitioners.

Several studies have taken place which identify the best strategies to raise the attainment of 'Black boys' (Blair 2001; OFSTED 2002a; Weekes and Wright 1998). A more recent publication we found particularly useful is *The Mouchel Parkman Report: Raising the Attainment of Black Boys* (2003) which spells out four key principles of good practice:

- A culture of high expectation.

- Respect, recognition and an understanding of the multiple needs and identities of 'Black boys'.

- Support and access to a broad, balanced and inclusive pre- and post-16 curriculum.

- Partnership working with parents.

More specifically, this requires

- Understanding the multiple identities of Black and minority ethnic (bme) boys (racial, cultural, gender, adolescent).

- Integrating this knowledge into policies, practice, the curriculum and a whole-school ethos.

- Providing interactive and group-orientated learning and teaching styles.

- Monitoring of attainment and behaviour by gender and ethnicity.

- Developing positive relationships between pupils, teachers and parents.

- Implementing clear and consistent behaviour policies that explicitly address racism.

(Based on *The Mouchel Parkman Report* 2003).

We will be exploring many of the themes raised in *The Mouchel Parkman Report* later in this chapter, but at this point we consider the issue of multiple or overlapping factors of identity, namely social class, gender and ethnicity.

What's class got to do with it?

'Social class' or the socio-economic position of people in society (Gidden 2001) has a bearing on their access to public services such as education and health, their financial situation and their future prospects in the labour market. If you take social class as a determinant of inequality, Weekes and Wright (1998) found that 'inequalities of attainment are now evident for Black pupils regardless of their social class background' (1998: 20). Moreover

> social class factors do not override the influence of ethnic inequality: when comparing pupils with similar class background there are still marked inequalities of attainment between different ethnic groups. (ibid: 21)

Whilst targeting social class disadvantage is necessary, treated in isolation it is likely to have a limited effect in closing the gap between different ethnic groups. Weekes and Wright also state that the gender gap is considerably smaller than the inequalities associated with ethnic origin and social class background, but as part of a collective identity 'Black boys' are documented as being a key group of academic under-achievers.

And the gender Issue?

As we saw at the beginning of this chapter, concern has been expressed over the positioning of African Caribbean boys (Sewell 1996, 2007), and indeed boys in general because of their consistent under-achievement at all stages of their education (DfES 2006a). Achievement according to gender shows that boys in general have been under-achieving compared to girls since 1998: for example, 66.3 per cent of girls achieved 5 A*–C grades at GCSE in maintained schools in 2005, compared to 60 per cent of boys (DfES 2006a).

If you combine ethnic background and gender as factors in consideration of under-achievement, and in some cases social class, Black African Caribbean and Pakistani/Bangladeshi boys may be particularly vulnerable to under-achievement.

Time to reflect

◆ In what ways is your teaching responsive to the issues raised above in terms of ethnic background and gender?

◆ How does this relate to under-achievement within your own school context?

Terms – what's in a word?

Before we look at issues and strategies concerning the under-achievement of 'Black boys', we need to clarify our terminology further and highlight the complexity of issues involved for practitioners.

Ethnicity is about how people define themselves and the concept relates to a wide range of very diverse groups, for example Sikhs, Bengalis, Pakistanis and those from African and Caribbean communities. 'Ethnicity' is a factor which can help give people a sense of belonging and which provides both individuals and groups with a shared sense of identity. Within this chapter, our focus is on Black African and Caribbean, Pakistani and Bangladeshi learners because collectively they account for the largest group of minority ethnic pupils (Gillborn and Mirza 2000; DfES 2006a and b.)

As we discussed earlier in Chapter 1, the word 'Black' or 'Asian' is sometimes used as convenient shorthand to cover a range of pupils but it can obscure differences within and among these groups. As such, 'Black' is used generically to include boys of African and Caribbean background and those of dual heritage or mixed race. Similarly, 'Asian' is used generically to include those pupils of South East Asian heritage, for example Pakistani or Bangladeshi. However, as we noted in Chapter 1, the term has been criticized because it ignores the huge differences in culture within these diverse groups (Modood et al. 1997). Also, if we look at the format of the 2001 Census, the term 'Black' is divided further into:

- Black.

- Black Caribbean.

- Black African.

- Black other.

As with the term 'Asian', 'Black African' also includes diverse groups, for example, Zimbabwean, Congolese and Somalian, with potentially different educational needs.

We should also note that we use the phrase 'Black boys' cautiously, not just because of the wide range of ethnic groups subsumed within this category, but also because of the use of the term 'boys'. The word 'boy' is significant in the power hierarchy within Black culture: 'men' may be esteemed, but not 'boys', and gaining respect whilst still of school age can be of importance to some members of this group of learners. Sewell (2007) maintains that if we are trying to understand the attainment of 'Black boys' we need to consider issues of male gender and masculinity, what it is to be a male adolescent, and importantly, the impact of peer pressure which may make academic pursuit seem 'uncool'. This can be seen within the context of young males' understanding of 'masculinity' and the varied, and at times negative, ways in which this can have meaning (Connolly 2003; Skelton 2001). For example, the concept of 'negative masculinity' is examined in *Being a Real Man in Islam* as follows:

> negative masculinity is about showing off, about trying to be 'hard', and about using physical strength to humiliate others ... negative masculinity is about wasting time like a child. He looks out for himself first, neither respecting the wishes of his parents nor serving them, and ignoring the needs of others around him (Birt 2001).

There may be shared notions of masculinity among all male adolescents. Further, whilst there are some common strategies applicable to boys in general, we also need to caution against assuming that 'one size-fits-all': there are some cultural and religious issues which may have significance to specific groups, for example flexibility in the timetable to accommodate Friday prayers for Muslim pupils – an issue we will return to later in this chapter.

From the discussion so far, we can see that some pupils have overlapping issues of identity involving ethnicity, gender and religion. Cultural diversity is ever changing and the terminology we use to describe different groups is dynamic and capable of constant refinement. We have tried to reflect this in our glossary, and there are some useful websites which contain up-to-date glossaries on key terms, for example:

- multiverse provides information and resources for teachers, students and trainees on diversity in the classroom (www.multiverse.ac.uk).

- insted is a DfES funded site which explores anti-racist teaching (www.insted.co.uk/raise.html).

- britkid provides discussion on race, racism and life as seen by young people (www.britkid.org).

- Eurokid is an antiracist and intercultural website exploring issues of identity and racism from the perspectives of students in Spain, Sweden and Britain (www.eurokid.org).

Minority ethnic groups

As we noted at the beginning of the book, terminology has shifted from 'ethnic minority' to 'minority ethnic' (Dadzie 2000), which suggests the inclusion of all groups in society, visible or non-visible in terms of skin colour or ethnicity. Some writers talk about 'minority groups' which broadens out the discussion and can be applied to a range of groups within a school, based on such factors as religion, language, disability, gender or sexual orientation. There is, however, a danger of labelling pupils with stereotypical assumptions as to their strengths and weaknesses. Further, although 'ethnic monitoring' on the basis of the presence of minority ethnic groups can help a school maintain an accurate record of academic attainment rather than an image or perception, we need to remember that each child is an individual and will have different experiences and views of school. (We return to this important point later in the chapter when we look at a case study of effective practice.)

Multiple senses of identity

From the discussion so far we have highlighted individual and overlapping descriptors which suggest that pupils do not have a single form of personal identification but multiple senses of identity, for example:

- Black.

- 'Asian'.

- Boy.

- Middle/working class.

As we noted above, the term 'Black' can also include individuals of mixed race or dual heritage (Tizard and Phoenix 2002). For some pupils identity may be seen in terms of colour (Rattansi 2000), for others their cultural heritage and especially their religion may be the main markers of identity (Modood 2003). A child's perception of how they are seen by others was strongly expressed during one of our earlier studies, when a Muslim girl said 'We're always Asian, Miss, never British' (Parker-Jenkins and Haw 1996).

An important task for teachers is to be aware of pupils' backgrounds and to engage in inclusive education, to ensure all children feel welcome and have the opportunity to succeed. Practitioners also need to be aware of the hybridity or diversity of identities within Britain, and to be prepared to assist and support young people as they shape and test out mixed identities, as distinct from single identities:

> It follows that there are many ways of being a British Muslim or British Sikh, for example, just as there are many different ways of being a British Christian. (Richardson 2006)

We need to remember also that minority ethnic pupils who have a visible profile may feel unaccepted and unwelcome by the wider community even though they were born here, and can be subjected to racism. The debate on what counts as 'racism' became a key part of mainstream politics with the publication of the MacPherson Report (1999) into the murder of Black teenager Stephen Lawrence, which we highlighted earlier in Chapter one. The report is important for making clear that there can be 'unwitting' or unintentional racism:

> unwitting racism can arise because of lack of understanding, ignorance or mistaken beliefs. It can arise from well intentioned but patronising words or actions. It can arise from unfamiliarity with the behaviour or cultural traditions of people or families from minority ethnic communities. It can arise from racist stereotyping of black people as potential criminals or troublemakers (MacPherson Report 1999: 22).

Whilst racism may be classified as intentional or unintentional, the net result of 'unthinking racist insults' and 'unintentional stereotypical racial references' can have an impact on pupils (Pearce 2005). Some pupils have to deal with racism not due to the colour of their skin necessarily, but because of 'cultural racism' (Modood), based on their religion or cultural background – a point we discuss later in the chapter with reference to the issue of 'Islamophobia'. Academic attainment, therefore, needs to be seen in the wider context of how pupils are treated in school by other members of the school community, and how well they are supported.

Activities – Cultural survey

In what ways are you made aware of the cultural and religious differences among your pupils? Think of your own school, and particularly the children in your class.

What are their cultural backgrounds?

What multiple identities do the pupils possess?

One approach used to support pupils from minority ethnic backgrounds is to invite into schools adults from the same cultural background to assist in both personal and academic development.

Mentoring

The term 'mentoring' is used in many walks of life today to describe a range of activities aimed at supporting individuals. Generally the roles and expectations of a mentoring system can be formally set out within an institutional plan, or alternatively mentoring can take place as an informal, ad hoc arrangement between individuals and schools (Fletcher 2000). There is a National Framework for mentoring and coaching, managed by the Teacher Development Agency, showcasing examples of good practice in educational institutions (CUREE 2006). In the mentor/mentee relationship within schools, the basic styles of helping are:

- To guide.

- To support.

- To advise.

- To enable.

- To empower.

(See Klasen and Clutterbuck 2002).

The use of mentors is a strategy being used on both sides of the Atlantic for Black and Asian 'boys' (Sewell 2007). The existence of positive, minority ethnic role models in schools at all levels from senior management to technical support could clearly benefit 'Black boys', but the ethnic composition of school staff is less than 5 per cent (DfES 2004). In the absence of appropriate role models, therefore, practitioners can explore mentoring possibilities involving adults from outside the school. There are a number of organizations adopting this approach to raise self-esteem and to support students both academically and in personal development. These include the following:

- The National Black Boys Can Association.

- Boys2Men.

- From Childhood to Manhood.

- Generating Genius.

Boys2Men, for example, provides role models from within the Black community and the organization sends male facilitators into primary schools to provide personal development support and mentoring (Children Now 2005). This use of mentoring as a strategy is a key issue in underachievement according to Sewell (2007):

> a lack of positive male role models, peer pressure, street culture and the notion that it's not cool to do well in school are all factors that contribute to low achievement in Black boys (ibid: 20).

To respond to this, Sewell has established an intervention strategy in the form of a 12-week, secondary-based programme called 'Generating Genius' to help support 'Black boys' and to turn around academic downturn (Sewell 2007). This use of mentoring assumes a long-term commitment on behalf of the mentor, ideally throughout the duration of a pupil's secondary school life. Another scheme is 'buddying-up' students with Black role models from the workplace – for example pharmacists, store managers, the military, and high-achieving members of the Black community – who come into schools to work with pupils (Children Now). In other words, the development of a critical mass of Black exemplars is being developed and encouraged to help 'Black boys' be successful in school. As part of this work, some schools have also formed Black male student groups with the view to raising attainment and self-esteem. Different localities have developed a Black achievement strategy with a number of roles to help schools, for example, Black Achievement Consultants, Achievement Mentors, and Black Inclusion Officers. School practitioners can link with such groups to support learning in the classroom.

Whilst the cause of 'Black boys" under-achievement is complex, teachers need to ensure that that they provide creative and motivating learning experiences, along with a curriculum which reflects the heritage, culture and experiences of Black and African Caribbean boys, and that they do not engage in discriminatory practices. Interestingly, 'Black boys' have reported that they experience sexism and that girls generally receive more positive teacher attention than boys (LDA 2004). This view is also borne out in our research, discussed later in this chapter, where the boys felt that girls were being treated more favourably in the classroom.

We know from research that in terms of pupil progress teachers should have detailed knowledge of each pupil's progress with broad assessment arrangements. These should include for example:

- An assessment portfolio.

- A homework policy.

- Regularly marked and graded work.

- Early identification of those pupils not making progress.

- Parental perspectives and support.

- An ethos that is open and vigilant, which enables pupils to discuss 'race' issues and share concerns.

- High expectations with a clear view that under-performance by any group is unacceptable.

- A review of curricular and pastoral approaches.

- Ethnic monitoring as a routine and rigorous part of the school's self-evaluation and management (Gillborn and Mirza 2000).

As part of understanding and assessing pupils' work you need also to identify opportunities to discuss progress and achievement with them, in a manner appropriate to their age, and on a small or one-to-one basis.

Time to reflect

How do you identify ability and celebrate success.

Think about your own classroom practice and write down ways in which you make arrangements for assessment and celebrate the success of male pupils:

1

2

3

4

Activites – Listening to pupils

How do you arrange to listen to your pupils, to explore issues and to set/negotiate targets? Make a list of five points and compare your thinking with that of a colleague's – is your practice similar or different in approach?

1

2

3

4

5

The inclusive curriculum

One of the ongoing issues about responding to cultural diversity and raising academic attainment is the adequacy of the curriculum. Prior to the introduction of the National Curriculum (DfES 1989), work had been done on moving away from:

- An ethnocentric curriculum that is the application of the norms of your own culture to that of others (Brown 1965).

- A Eurocentric curriculum, namely placing White European and/or American males as the norm, and as the sole contributors to such things as scientific discovery (Guttman 1992).

There is still room within the National Curriculum to find opportunities to identify and celebrate the achievement of others, and to think about the selection of resources you use in the classroom. For example, try exploring Asian and Black History in Britain 1500–1850 using Black and Asian History websites (www.blackpresence; www.bbc.multicultural history at Key Stage 4; www.channel4blackandasian history). The website on '100 Great Black Britons'

Awareness of Black History

Did you know, for example, that England has had two black queens (see www.100great-blackbritons)?

Think of the curriculum you use in the classroom.

Where is there inclusion of Black history and culture in your teaching, displays, festivals, music, literature, drama?

What do you know about the contribution of Black scientists, historians and writers?

List:

- three Black writers;
- three Black scientists;
- three Black historians.

showcases Black achievements and contributions over the centuries (www.100greatblackbritons). Similarly, Islam's contribution to science and technology is well presented on the '1001 Inventions' website (www.1001inventions.com). Here Muslim heritage in the world is demonstrated in an accessible way with reference to Muslim contributions to the home, the world of education, medicine, and art. (We return to this point later in the chapter when we look at supporting pupils of Pakistani and Bangladeshi background.)

Case studies as illustrations of effective practice

Not all boys from minority ethnic backgrounds are under-achieving and in some schools 'Black boys' and those of Asian heritage are 'bucking the trend' of under-attainment as documented by the DfES (2003a). Research has also been carried out in *The Mouchel Parkman Report* (2003a) using schools in Nottingham and Birmingham.

As part of our work in identifying and promoting good practice in raising the academic attainment of 'Black boys', we carried out our own research project. We also chose schools in the Midlands area where there was quantifiable proof of academic attainment and we conducted one in-depth case study to explore why 'Black boys' were performing well academically. Our case study school could be described as an 'attaining school' because it has specific policy, goals and strategies, and sets store on all pupils achieving their full potential. For the purpose of our discussion we focus on the practice we observed which could be useful in specifically targeting the achievement of boys from minority ethnic backgrounds.

Background

Mainland Community School is an 11–18 co-ed on the outskirts of a Midlands city with 1278 pupils, and was established in 1949, with a purpose-built sixth-form centre added in 2000. The school demonstrates strong leadership from senior management, with an ethos of being an achieving school in which all children can and will succeed academically: this is announced very clearly at the school's open days and Year 7 briefings. At parents' evenings, the head-teacher makes clear the school's position on non-authorized absences, with particular reference to prolonged absence for holidays or visits abroad to extended families.

As well as providing a system in which pupils' ethnic and religious backgrounds are understood – a system in which the pupils all do matter and do count – there are creative ways of recognizing and rewarding different types of success, especially with older pupils. For example, for those with 100 per cent attendance throughout the year, the headteacher collects these pupils in a limousine for a breakfast celebration at a local hotel!

Even when we allowed for socio-economic factors, the Years 10 and 11 boys of Black Caribbean, and minority ethnic background (mostly Muslim) had achieved academic success in the school by comparison with DfES figures. They had sufficient pass grades at GCSE to permit entrance to the school's sixth form centre.

When we interviewed these male students about positive strategies and barriers to successful post-14 learning, we found the following key pointers:

Successful Strategies	*Barriers/Difficulties*

The Curriculum

■ A variety of activities within lessons	■ Copying out of textbook
■ Plenty of examples given	■ Repeated subjects
■ The use of ICT in teaching	■ Irrelevance of topics
■ Allowing for pupils to model and teach the class	■ Every lesson the same
■ Relevant topics and material used	

The Teachers

■ Two-way respect	■ Nicer to girls than boys
■ Warm and approachable	■ Compare you to others
■ Positively challenge you	■ Distrust you
■ Praise you in front of others	■ Don't listen to your side of the story
■ Variation in pace of lessons	■ Feeling of not being liked by the teachers
■ Playing the radio as pupils work	

The Classroom

■ Nice facilities (desks and computers)	■ Absence of clocks
■ Different classrooms for different lessons	■ Sitting one per table
■ Bright displays	■ Classrooms too hot
■ Comfortable chairs	■ Inadequate lockers

Resources

■ Use of SMART Boards	■ Old or disintegrating textbooks
■ OHP	■ Lots of writing
■ Computer software	

From our research findings cited above, it is important to note that the school was able to evidence under-achievement using Data Power computer software packages by which teachers could 'track' a pupil's grades in all subjects and detect a rise or decline in achievement and/or a pattern of declining under-achievement. This then allowed staff to use an intervention approach to try and halt a downward spiral. The introduction of the Pupil Level Annual School Census in 2001 and the development of the National Pupil Database (NDP) whereby all schools supply data to the DfES using the same ethnic coding have together meant that accurate information on ethnicity and gender can now be obtained. In addition, the web-based system, Reporting and Analysis for Improvement through School Self-Evaluation (RAISE Online 2006), produced by OFSTED and the DfES, helps support schools self–evaluation and for tracking the progress of pupils on an individual basis (see www.raiseonline.org).

Another issue which emerged from this case study focusing on boys achievement which has also been observed elsewhere (Rowan et al. 2002) is that it is important to ensure that a variety of teaching approaches is used, and that there should be a mix between learning styles, namely:

- Auditory.

- Visual.

- Kinaesthetic.

- Digital.

In *Boys Literacies and Schooling*, Rowan et al. (2002) argue that the failure of many boys to achieve basic literacy levels is tied to a broad, school-based culture of defeat, and that we need to ensure that boys' learning needs are reflected in our teaching approach. Bite-size or boy-size chunks of information which are modelled by the teacher were also cited as a preferred style of learning. Likewise, activities concerning 'brain gym' (www.learning-solutions.co.uk) and 'Active 8' (www.nationwidechildcare.co.uk), supported by physical activities, can be of use. In the case study school, the overall impression we received from the sixth form students was that the institution was 'boy-friendly' in terms of the environment and teaching styles.

Activities – Boys' learning styles

Think of your own school situation.

Is there a pattern of which boys are achieving and which are under-achieving?

What is their preferred learning style?

How do you know for sure? Is this carefully monitored?

What do you do already? For boys in general? For boys from a minority ethnic background?

Reflect on the list you have created as you engage with the remainder of the chapter, considering how you could adapt your current practice and/or introduce new strategies..

Intervention programmes

From the case study above it was clear that the school was systematically collecting the pupil scores and using a software package to track the progress of each pupil from Year 7 – to identify the point at which achievement rose or declined, to monitor the pattern and to make appropriate intervention decisions in the event of under-performance or a downward spiral emerging. In the event of a decline in academic performance, the school approached a pupil's parents or carers through the Head of Year and/or a member of staff responsible for home–school relations. Regular contact with the home, and additional school support and/or mentoring, formed part of the intervention strategy. The impact of this approach worked towards ensuring that the pupil's progress generally improved. Indeed, Mainland School achieved academic results in SATs levels well above the national and regional average. This strategy and support were set within the ethos of being 'an attaining school' with high expectations of all pupils as noted above, and the target of a 100 per cent success rate of pupils having five GCSEs at Level C or above.

There is a range of early intervention strategies available for teachers to adopt at a classroom, school, local and national level. All of these support the idea that when teachers, parents and the wider community are involved they can have a positive impact on the achievement of pupils, but the earlier they are introduced and the longer they continue the greater the potential benefit to pupils. We look at the involvement of parents and the wider community later in Chapter 6, but at this point we consider using other schools as examples of 'good practice' or as a potential resource. *The Mouchel Parkman Report* on raising the attainment of 'Black boys' (2003), noted earlier, highlights a range of strategies within a matrix of good practice. One of the strategies identified was 'networking with successful schools' to help raise academic attainment.

Activites – Work with other schools

Talk with colleagues in your school or LA about any projects which focus on the under-achievement of boys and/or those of a minority ethnic background. Consider which programmes could be adapted to support and extend your current practice.

For example, a mentoring programme could be introduced as an important way to support and inspire pupils (Sewell 2007).

Alternatively, an event to celebrate Black heroes and heroines with the whole community could be arranged.

So far we have focused on 'Black boys' from African and Caribbean backgrounds, but as we said at the beginning of this chapter, another key group of under-achievers is boys of Asian heritage, namely those of Pakistani and Bangladeshi backgrounds. The discussion now moves to look at ways in which this group of learners can be supported, and how identity on the basis of religion can have a bearing on how pupils see themselves and are treated.

British Pakistani and Bangladeshi learners

I wish teachers knew a little about my background so that they have a better understanding of my religious and cultural beliefs. Not necessary too much in depth. Just enough to know something about me (Year 11 boy at a school in Sheffield, RAISE 2004: 39).

The RAISE project was set up in 2002 by the Uniting Britain Trust, in association with the Churches Regional Commission and with the involvement of a number of local education authorities, to raise the under-achievement of Pakistani and Kashmiri pupils. (National statistics refer to this group of learners within the single term of 'Pakistani'.) Local authorities involved in the initiative included Birmingham, Bradford, Leeds, Leicester, Sheffield and Slough. The RAISE study uses a triangle motif to suggest the idea that young British Pakistani people grow up with three major influences:

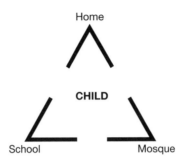

Interestingly, you will notice that the lines of the triangle are broken – this is to signify that connections need to be built and at a number of levels within the wider social, national and global context. In terms of our discussion here, this project is helpful in informing knowledge on a number of fronts:

- British Pakistanis are not a single, homogeneous unit but a community of communities.

- Whilst the majority of British Pakistanis and Bangladeshis are Muslim, they vary in their religious practice as do members of other religious groups.

- A substantial proportion of Pakistani communities in the West Midlands and the North originated from Azad Kashmir in Pakistan and being Kashmiri is an important part of their cultural history and sense of personal identity (RAISE 2004).

A further important issue is that not all pupils of Pakistani origin are under-achieving: the academic level in the West Midlands and the North is generally low, but in London and the South East their educational achievement is on a par or higher than the national average. For example, in 2004, 53 per cent of pupils of Pakistani background in London achieved five A*–C grades, higher than the national average, but those in the North West, West Midlands, Yorkshire and Humber varied between 34 and 41 per cent, with girls outperforming boys. Importantly, Pakistani girls are generally achieving well, for example 62.1 per cent achieved A*–C at GCSE in maintained schools in 2005, compared with 52.4 per cent of Pakistani boys (www.dfes.gov.uk/rsgateway). This suggests that gender and not ethnicity is the key issue.

In terms of language usage, most Pakistani children learn English as an additional language, and as we saw earlier in Chapter 3, a number of projects such as Talking Partners in Bradford (www.educationbradford.com) and the 'English in the Mainstream' course developed in Australia have been used to assist in the acquisition of English, particularly for newly arrived learners.

The 2001 Census is useful for additional information about Pakistani learners. It shows that Pakistani communities in the North and the West Midlands suffer from unemployment, poverty and social exclusion, and DfES figures demonstrate that almost 40 per cent of Pakistani pupils in secondary schools are eligible for free school meals, compared with a national average of around 15 per cent. However, as stated above, we need to be cautious when attempting to adequately describe different groups, bearing in mind such factors as social class (Ali et al 2006). One fact which emerges from the literature (Modood 2003; Knowles and Ridley 2006), however, and from our own research is that many of the strategies to raise achievement are applicable to all pupils:

> there is .. a need for measures that take explicit account of British Muslim identity, and the history, experience and perceptions of British Pakistani communities. A difference-blind approach is not sufficient (Richardson 2006).

In terms of learning and teaching, there are opportunities within the National Curriculum to acknowledge and celebrate the contribution that Islam has made to the culture of the world, for example through:

- Calligraphy.

- Islamic art.

- Islamic contributions to mathematics and science.

A sensitive approach to teaching about the Crusades and the promotion of positive role models in Islamic cultural tradition have all been advocated for the last two decades (Dufour 1990): in other words, in addition to the promotion of Western values, the inclusion of a wide variety of learning experiences and opportunities in all subject areas drawing on other cultural groups.

Engaging in a broad and varied curriculum can involve using the pupil background as a starting point, and utilizing the religious, cultural and linguistic heritages, not as a kind of tokenism but as a springboard for learning, teaching and assessment which all pupils can share (Ofsted 2002a and b).

Time to reflect – Pupils' sense of identity

As we have noted in this discussion, pupils may have a sense not just of dual identity but also of multiple senses of identity. This is well-captured by the following quote:

> I could view myself as a member of the following communities depending on the context and in no particular order: Black, Asian, Azad Kashmiri, Mirpuri, Jat, Marilail, Kungriwalay, Pakistani, English, British, Yorkshire man, Bradfordian, from Bradford Moor … I could use the term 'community' in any of these contexts and it would have meaning. Any attempt to define me only as one of these would be meaningless. (Richardson and Wood 2004: 4)

Look at the above list of identities and consider:

- How many as a teacher do you recognize?

- How many are new to you?

- How many are shared by pupils in your school?

A similar project to RAISE is the Raising Achievement of Pakistani/Bangladeshi Boys Project (RAPBB) in Birmingham. One of the things this project acknowledged was that the majority of its pupils attended supplementary schools or *madrassahs* and this was seen as an integral part of their development as Muslims (Parker-Jenkins et al. 2005). (Similarly, supplementary schools for African and Caribbean children which take place in the evening or at weekends focus on both academic success and building self-esteem.) In terms of Muslim pupils, mosques are also a place where they may feel a sense of being Muslim, where they have the opportunity to learn Arabic and Islamic texts and celebrate *Jumu'ah* or Friday congregational prayers (Sarwar 1994), and where they may share experiences of 'Islamophobia'.

'Islamophobia'

Pupils of Pakistani and Bangladeshi backgrounds may suffer from religious bigotry as well as racism. In British society and elsewhere in the West, anti-Muslim prejudice has become more explicit and more pervasive. Islamophobia is defined as

> unfounded hostility towards Islam, and therefore fear or dislike of all or most Muslims. (Runnymede Trust 1997).

Features of Islamophobia include:

- Verbal and physical attacks on Muslims.

- Attacks on mosques and desecration of Muslim cemeteries.

- Widespread and routine negative stereotyping in the media.

- Discrimination in recruitment and employment practices.

- Lack of attention to the fact that Muslims in Britain are disproportionately affected by poverty and social exclusion (van Driel 2004).

In such a climate, younger generations of British Muslims may well feel alienated and disaffected, and that they are not accepted or welcomed by other members of society. As we saw in relation to the issue of racism earlier, this can have an impact on children's well-being:

> Islamophobia can have the effect of undermining young people's self-confidence and self-esteem (Richardson and Wood 2004: 13).

In terms of the implications for practitioners, this does not mean 'that all aspects of Islam are beyond criticism', (Richardson 2006), but that discussion and disagreements should be respectful and informed. It is also worth noting that some pupils may belong to a religious group by way of their own choice and/or that of their parents, and as such, practitioners need to develop 'religious literacy' as well as cultural awareness:

> religious literacy … includes understanding and taking seriously secular and humanist beliefs as well as religious ones (Richardson 2006).

Activities – Encouraging mutual respect

Consider how you as a teacher promote mutual respect and provide an atmosphere of openness and tolerance in your teaching and in your classroom.

Outside of school, pupils may have links with *imams*, mosques and *madrassahs*. To what extent might these connections help you inform your own knowledge and understanding?

How might you work in closer partnership with these groups in teaching pupils you both share?

As we mentioned earlier, involving members of the community as mentors can be a useful strategy to support learners. Initiatives have taken place amongst 'Asian' groups to implement this strategy. For example, in Project Proactive members of a Pakistani Centre aim to recruit three Muslim mentors each month to work with adolescent Muslim boys (www.nottingham-schools.co.uk/ems). Similarly, there are schemes to provide mentoring for both Black and Asian boys, which involve recruiting Black, Asian and Pakistani volunteers to work in local schools (www.gos.gov.uk/goem). There is also an attempt within this initiative to respond to the cultural and generational differences between 'Asian' groups, for as we noted earlier in the book, cultural diversity in the classroom is changing and educational needs reflect this diversity. As such, some newly arrived refugee and asylum seeker children from Pakistan have language support needs not shared by third or fourth generation British Pakistani pupils. It is important for practitioners to carefully select strategies which are appropriate for the age group and background of the pupils. As one strategy, you could approach Ethnic Minority Achievement Grant staff who have been tasked to introduce and support initiatives.

New initiatives such as mentoring are being used to help reverse the trend of under-achievement (Kirsh 2005). As well as involving role models in teaching activities for Black pupils, 'Asian' representation in teaching and teaching support should also be advocated. Asian professionals can also be encouraged to provide work experience and placement opportunities for your pupils. (We look at using the community as a resource later in Chapter 6).

Key Points

■ Black and minority ethnic boys are reported as among the lowest achievers in schools.

■ It is important to understand different key terms concerning social class, ethnicity and gender.

■ Some pupils may have multiple senses of identity.

■ Good practice is reflected in monitoring progress, the curriculum, teaching styles and classroom settings.

■ Effective monitoring of progress with feedback mechanisms and celebration of success are excellent strategies for raising attainment.

■ Understanding 'Islamophobia' and recognizing its negative impact on self-esteem are essential topics of discussion for all practitioners to be aware of.

■ There are similar issues and strategies that can be used to assist Black and Caribbean and African boys, and those of 'Asian' heritage, such as the use of an inclusive curriculum which acknowledges cultural achievement and a contribution to knowledge, community mentoring, and liaising with supplementary schools and *madrassahs*.

In Chapter 5 we explore strategies for what has been classified as the lowest group of under-achievers, that of Gypsy, Roma and Traveller children in the UK.

CHAPTER 5

Gypsy, Roma and Traveller children in the UK

This chapter looks at:

- traveller family, community and gender issues

- admissions

- anti-bullying and anti-racism

- behaviour, communication and the peer group

- the curriculum

- attendance.

I think all travelling children should go to school, they will learn a lot more than staying in one place and not getting out. They need to get an education because the world is changing. They need to know how to read and write, so they can deal with people every day (Father of Gypsy/Traveller children, Bhopal 2004: 54).

These are positive words but this community has been described as 'probably the most deprived group of the country' (DES 1967). In 1996b OFSTED said that as many as 50,000 children between the ages of 5 and 16 years were registered in school at that time, whilst 10,000 were not. In a follow-up report in 1999a OFSTED also explained that Gypsy, Roma and Traveller children were amongst the least achieving groups.

Look at the following questions to reflect on your own knowledge and attitudes towards the Gypsy, Roma and Traveller community.

Activities – First thoughts

Explore your intial ideas on Gypsy, Roma and Traveller children:

- Do you have any of these children in your school?

▶

■ What do you know of their community and culture?

■ What are the best ways to support and teach Gypsy, Roma and Traveller children?

■ Why is the achievement of Gypsy, Roma and Traveller children poor in some schools?

Background

O'Hanlon and Holmes (2004) explain that the terms 'Gypsy' and 'Traveller' are used to cover a range of different ethnic, cultural and occupational groups. In a book for children called *The Travelling People*, Wormington et al. (2003) explain that Gypsies first originated in India around about 1000 AD. In fact the term 'Gypsy' comes from 'Egyptian'. People wrongly thought that the Gypsies came from Egypt.

There are many different groups of people who might be called Gypsies or Travellers, such as:

■ Travellers of Irish, Scottish, and Welsh Heritage.

■ Romany Gypsies from England and Wales.

■ Roma Gypsies from Eastern Europe (Romany people).

■ New Age Travellers.

■ Bargee Travellers.

■ Circus Travellers.

■ Showground (showpeople) Travellers.

If you have realized here that Circus and Showground Travellers (showpeople) are an occupational group, then you were right. Many of them prefer the term 'Traveller'. They may originate from the British Isles or could more recently have entered the country as a refugee (for example, the Roma Gypsies of Eastern Europe).

> My children tell me that the other kids call them names. They call them 'dirty, smelly gypos' and that hurts us because we're not dirty or smelly. But that is something we have to put up with, because we're seen as being different. We don't live in houses and people make judgments about us, which are always bad and negative Bhopal (2004: 55).

Everyone has prejudice in them if they are honest. Developing your understanding of Gypsy, Roma and Traveller communities and cultures will help you to identify prejudice in yourself. The first step in supporting Gypsy, Roma and Traveller communities is to understand that they comprise a variety of ethnic groups.

Travellers of Irish heritage, like many nomadic ethnic groups, have usually operated on the margins of the job market: for example, laying tarmac, breaking up cars for scrap and tree lopping. They are largely Roman Catholic, often seeking to place their children in faith schools of their religion (O'Hanlon and Holmes 2004).

Romany Gypsies have many similarities with Irish Travellers. Each group has a language or dialect of its own. You will recognize some Romani words from popular culture. Many have been taken into English (O'Hanlon and Holmes 2004). Irish Travellers use elements of old languages often described as Gammon or Shelter.

Romani Words

dai	–	mother
dadrus	–	father
mush	–	man
kusthi	–	good

Other background issues include:

- Bargee Travellers who live on barges and travel on the canals and waterways.

- Roma Gypsies who come from the East of Europe: the Czech Republic, the former USSR, the Balkans and Greece. They suffered significantly at the hands of the Nazis in the Second World War and whole villages of Roma Gypsies were exterminated in the concentration camps. The English themselves were responsible for persecuting Gypsies long before the Nazis. Edward VI passed a law which required all Gypsies to be branded and made into slaves for two years. 1650 was the last year in which someone was executed 'for the crime of being a Gypsy' (O'Hanlon and Holmes 2004).

- Showground and Circus Travellers have been visiting part of the country for many centuries with fairs or more recently circus shows. Many Roma groups have been associated with theatre and music performance. Django Rheinhart, for example, was a famous jazz musician from the mid-twentieth century who played a guitar with just two fingers on his left hand: the result of a fire in his Gypsy caravan (O'Hanlon and Holmes 2004).

- New Age Travellers differ from other Gypsy and Traveller groups as they cannot be identified by basing this on their ethnicity or occupation. For many, to become a New Age Traveller is a lifestyle choice: rejecting modern and urban ways of living in some cases for a more environmentally friendly approach. New Age families have been particularly affected by recent legislation (O'Hanlon and Holmes 2004). (This is summarized below).

- There are approximately 350,000 people in the Gypsy, Roma and Traveller community, of whom many live in housing. A large number still live a travelling lifestyle: some live on local authority or privately owned caravan sites (Clark and Greenfields 2006). However, about 70,000 Travellers move around the country from one unauthorized encampment to another. Finding somewhere to site a caravan can be a major problem for Gypsy, Roma and Traveller families. In 1968 the Caravan Sites Act required local authorities to provide sites for

Gypsies and Travellers and their caravans but in 1984 the Criminal Justice and Public Order Act repealed this law. New legislation allowed the eviction of unlawful encampments (O'Hanlon and Holmes 2004).

Activities – Teaching Gypsy, Roma and Traveller children

Look at the following statements about the education of Gypsy, Roma and Traveller children. Do you agree with the statements? Do any of these relate to your own experience of working with Gypsy, Roma and Traveller children?

'It can be frustrating for the teacher when families move on unexpectedly.'

'I don't have the specialist knowledge to teach these children.'

'I find that Traveller and Gypsy families mistrust teachers and schools.'

'Gypsy boys can be quick to resort to violence if they feel undermined or are subject to name-calling.'

In fact all of these statements may be true for teachers and the Traveller children they teach. There is no one approach or method of working with Gypsy, Roma and Traveller children which is guaranteed to work, as is the case in so many areas of education. Trust, commitment and understanding are essential qualities for teachers and schools. There has been some research into the most effective approaches and these will be explained later in this chapter.

OFSTED (1996b, 1999a, 1999b) explained how Gypsy, Roma and Traveller children were not making progress in their education. Despite some evidence of improvement in the Primary years, it was said that:

- Attendance generally was still poor: in 1996 as many as 10,000 Gypsy, Roma and Traveller children were not attending school at any one time.

- Progress in learning was still poor in 1999 compared with 1996, especially in English.

- Exclusions of Gypsy, Roma and Traveller pupils were disproportionately high compared with non-Traveller pupils in the evidence collected by OFSTED.

- 74 per cent of Gypsy, Roma and Traveller children were on the Special Educational Needs register.

We can see from this that there was great concern about the educational achievements of Gypsy, Roma and Traveller pupils. Since the late 1990s there has been some research into what really works when helping Gypsy, Roma and Traveller children to do better in primary and secondary schools (DfES 2003b). It can be summarized as follows:

- Developing an approach to induction for newly arrived pupils, which addresses social as well as academic needs.

- Developing an inclusive and welcoming atmosphere by raising the profile of 'race' and equal opportunites in school.

- Involving Traveller parents and the wider community.

- Lifting barries to inclusion by developing a responsive and relevant curriculum.

- Working closely with the local authority's Travellers Education Support Service.

- Systematically monitoring the educational progress of Gypsy and Traveller children and building related targets into a school's action planning.

Traveller family, community and gender issues

In the next section you will find out more about how Gypsy, Roma and Traveller parents and pupils feel about school. Try to avoid the stereotypes which are sometimes associated with Gypsies, Roma and Travellers, one of which is that Gypsy. Roma and Traveller parents are not interested in their children's education. You will see in the following extracts that this is far from the case.

Case Study – Two points of view

Some of the things the children learn, they don't need to know about. Reading and writing, that's all they need. Above that, it's not important. Travelling children stick to their own tradition, my children want to stay with the community. Have you ever known a Gypsy barrister? I haven't. They never get that far and some of them don't need it, they have their own families who can take care of them. Mrs. Kennedy, mother of Traveller children (Bhopal: 53).

Now I've left I miss school. I hated it then. But now with two kids and a missus to scavenge for. At school I had no worries. It was a laugh. The kids took the p*** and all that, called us names. We never took no notice; well, sometimes, if they got too cocky, me and my two cousins kicked their heads in. I don't 'ave any grudges against them. Sorted it out when we were kids … Duke, former pupil and now parent of Traveller family (Levinson and Sparkes 2003: 592).

In the above quotes what do Gypsy, Roma and Traveller parents and children say about the following points:

- Important areas for learning?

- Bullying and ways of responding?

- Aspirations and expectations of success at school and for career prospects?

Keep these thoughts in mind as you read the following pages, which will explain in greater detail Gypsy, Roma and Traveller families and their approach to education.

The above quotes from the Gypsy, Roma and Traveller community illustrate some of their feelings in respect of education. Gypsies, Roma and Travellers clearly differ in their expectations about the importance of education and there is a fundamental tension here for Gypsy, Roma and Traveller communities. This is illustrated in the following diagram:

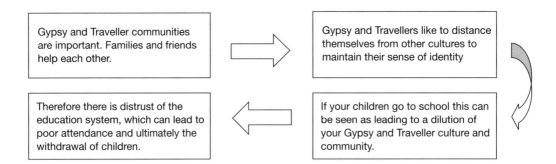

It would be wrong to paint a single view of Gypsy, Roma and Traveller families and schooling. As stated previously there is great variety in the Gypsy, Roma and Traveller communities. One parent summarized the feeling of marginalization and tension surrounding the education of her children:

> A lot of Travellers don't want to send their children to school. They think there's drugs and things out there. The parents are scared themselves because they didn't go to school. I'm glad I went to school and I encouraged my children as much as I could. I'm glad my daughter is going to school. Things are changing now in the Travelling world for the younger ones, maybe they will be going to school. Mrs Lindsay, parent (Bhopal 2004: 53).

Bhopal (2004) explains the unease of the Gypsy, Roma and Traveller community in their own words and it is important that we understand communities from their own perspective. For instance, O'Hanlon and Holmes (2004) explain the rituals and taboos of Gypsy families which are akin to Hindu rules on cleanliness. For instance, even though modern caravans could easily be equipped with modern toilets, many Gypsy families prefer not to have them in the caravan as this is seen as being 'unclean'. Different containers are used for cooking and cleaning so as not to break the rules of 'cleanliness'. Only a handful of Travellers live in a traditional horse-drawn caravan (*vardo*). However, a preference for highly decorated objects, glass and shiney surfaces to make the most of space and light can be seen in more modern caravans or even in the homes of housed Gypsies, Roma and Travellers (O'Hanlon and Holmes 2004).

Time to reflect – Cleanliness in the classroom

◆ Imagine that you are the teacher of a Reception class.

◆ In some Reception classes, there will be easy access toilets adjacent to the class or at the back of the room,

Think about the discomfort that this might cause a young Gypsy, Roma or Traveller child who has been raised in the belief that the toilet and living area should be distanced from each other.

Similarly, as we saw earlier in Chapter 3, issues concerning the use of the toilet may emerge due to language difficulties or cultural connotations.

The family and caravan are central to the lives of Gypsy, Roma and Traveller children. Though space is limited in caravans children are expected to adhere to family rules, which allow life to go on in closed spaces. Outside the caravan they have the freedom to play and explore and Gypsy, Roma and Traveller children often learn alongside their parents and older siblings. The caravan and its site are together a place of informal learning and pupils learn like apprentices even from a young age. This is particularly important for boys (O'Hanlon and Holmes 2004).

Levinson and Sparkes (2003) have done much to enlighten the wider community about the life of Gypsy, Roma and Traveller boys and young men, explaining how and why they act as they do. Learning alongside older brothers, cousins and especially their fathers not only allows boys to develop practical skills, but is very important also in helping them to establish their masculinity. Whereas girls are seen as having a nurturant role within the family, this is not the case for boys. Julie (a 19 year old Traveller) explains the roles of girls:

> I was helping by the time I could walk. By the age of 8, I was doing a lot of cleaning at home. I mean that's natural, like. You can't get a boy to wash up: 'e'd grow up all puffified; woman-like (Levinson and Sparkes 2003: 597).

The important role of women in Gypsy, Roma and Traveller communities is highlighted by a fieldworker in Levinson and Sparke's (2003) research. They state that some Gypsy, Roma and Traveller young men are involved in 'violence, robbery and other criminal damage', ending up in prison. Whilst older men are 'a bit more stable', the result of this is a matriarchal society. However, where a father was present he had the ultimate authority on the majority of issues. Some mothers observe that it is the men who oppose change and find adaptation to changing circumstances more difficult (Levinson and Sparkes 2003).

If men do find change more difficult, perhaps they are the ones who have most to lose if children attend school with the resultant dilution of their culture. Levinson and Sparkes (2003) reported that Gypsy boys in their study sought to demonstrate the qualities held up as being important to Gypsy men. These were:

- Business skills.
- Physical strength.
- Loyalty.
- Sexual prowess and potency.

They also give the example of a boy of 10 years old who once reported to them that becoming a millionaire and demonstrating great sexual prowess (in so many words) were the height of his ambition.

Gypsy boys often develop their business acumen at a young age. Nathan (aged 12) talks in Levinson and Sparkes (2004) of the pleasure he got from exchanging some items from a tip for a CD-music player from a non-Gypsy pupil at school. Nathan took pleasure from doing a good deal and for 'getting one over' on a non-Gypsy. Families frequently explained that these skills were learned at home and not in school:

> They're learning more at home. Why waste time in school? They're going to have to fend for themselves one day. Alfie, aged 30 (Levinson and Sparkes 2003: 590).

Many men and boys also see fighting as a demonstration of masculinity (Levinson and Sparkes 2003). There are many inter-family feuds and as various members of families inter-marry such feuds spread. This is not merely violence for the sake of violence. In and out of school, boys see fighting as a way of establishing the pecking order. Where violence happens in school, this can also be a response to name-calling and racism. Both children and families see the use of violence in these circumstances as legitimate. We looked at gender from the perspective of 'Black boys' in the previous chapter. A question we should ask ourselves here is whether the features we have discussed above relate to being male, being a Gypsy or being a male Gypsy? The following table will help you reflect on this.

Whilst the above qualities may be espoused for boys and men, this does not reduce the threat which many Gypsy, Roma and Traveller communities see in engaging with the wider community by sending their children to school. Bhopal (2004) explains that many families are concerned, especially as children approach their teenage years about the perceived immoralities of non-Gypsy society, in particular the exposure to sex and drugs. It is important therefore that schools make the first contact with Traveller and Gypsy families a positive one. This begins with the admissions policy and procedures.

Admissions

We discussed admissions in Chapter 2 with respect to asylum seeker and refugee children. Here the focus is on Gypsy, Roma and Traveller children. There are great similarities between provision for Gypsy, Roma and Traveller children and others from a diverse background. Admitting and inducting children into the school can be traumatic for children and parents (DfES 2003b). It can set a very positive tone for future relationships or it can lead to distrust, poor attendance, conflict and ultimately a withdrawal from school. These are some of the ways to support children and their parents. In *Aiming High: Raising the Achievement of Gypsy and Traveller Pupils* (DfES 2003b) several approaches are discussed.

Activities – Gypsy boys and behaviour in school

From a teacher's point of view, how can the qualities celebrated by Gypsy males impact on the classroom?

Look at the following table.

■ What strategies from the list might help address each of the areas?

Qualities for Gypsy masculinity	Problems in school	Possible strategies in school
Business acumen	Irrelevance of the National Curriculum	Building a relevant curriculum i.e. links to business in the 14–19 curriculum
Physical strength	Fighting, violence and bullying	Developing an interest in sports
Loyalty	Inter-group fighting	Developing responsibility for younger bothers and sisters
Sexual prowess/potency	Teenage pregnancy	Sex education and support from sexual health services

What other strategies can be added?

The induction and admission of Gypsy, Roma and Traveller children

It helps when:

- Administrative staff are welcoming to parents and pupils and sensitively offer help with filling in forms if this is needed.

- Pupils have a labelled place to put their belongings and a place to keep work in advance of their arrival.

- The headteacher meets parents and pupils and explains school polices and procedures, especially pupil health and safety, bullying and race equality and agrees how the school and family will communicate, such as by mobile phone or through outreach Traveller Education Support staff.

- Pupils are given a buddy who will look after them at break times and explain school routines.

- Pupils are paired with others in the class who will offer peer support for curriculum access if needed.

- Targeted use is made of both Traveller Education Support Service staff and materials and school support staff to ensure that a class teacher is able to offer a pupil access to the ongoing curriculum as soon as is possible.

- A key 'named' person is designated for the Gypsy, Roma and Traveller children to contact about any issues which arise for them within or outside school.

- A sanctuary area is identified, to where pupils worried about bullying or harassment or overwhelmed by school pressures can retreat.

- Staff are fully informed of a pupil's situation and informal training may be given.

(DfES 2003b)

The above approaches are judged by members of the Gypsy, Roma and Traveller community to be more effective in developing trust in pupils and parents towards the school (Bhopal 2004).

One parent explained it like this:

> We trust the teachers and the school. They make sure everything's done so that we are happy. The school always involves you. The Gypsy, Roma and Traveller teacher will always get on the phone and tell you what's going on. Being told what's going on and being involved makes a big difference. Then you know they care about you and they care what you think. Their actions show that they care and want to help our children in school (Bhopal 2004: 56).

O'Hanlon and Holmes (2004) explain that the close family relationships of Gypsy, Roma and Traveller children should also be considered when admitting very young children to school. Extended family and older siblings are often involved in bringing up younger brothers or sisters. It might help to reduce family anxiety if older brothers or sisters are allowed to see their younger siblings throughout the day so that both sides are reassured that the other is all right.

Time to reflect – Helping younger children at Admission

At break and lunchtimes a room away from the chaos of the playground can give brothers and sisters at the start of their time in school the chance to acclimatize to the bustle of normal school life.

The experience of children from Gypsy, Roma and Traveller families may be very varied in different schools. Some children may be located in the same area and attend the same school for most of their lives. Others may have a very interrupted experience of schooling, moving from one place to another as jobs dictate: for instance, as is the case for Showground and Circus Travellers.

The Roma Gypsies who have come to England in the last decade provide in some cases a greater challenge as they may have entered the country as asylum seekers or economic migrants (O'Hanlon and Holmes 2004). (Refugees and asylum seekers were also discussed in Chapter 3, and the latter terms were explained earlier in Chapter 2). Depending on their original circumstances, some Roma Gypsies may have suffered great persecution and as a result Roma Gypsy children can be traumatized by this experience. Schools will, therefore, have to consider the emotional and physical needs of these children in addition to their learning needs.

Roma Gypsy children may never have attended a school before. If they have done in the past the experience may have been significantly different, including for example:

■ A different language.

■ Different areas of learning.

■ Different methods for learning.

■ Different class routines for behaviour.

It is not uncommon for teachers to be presented with this situation when a Roma Gypsy child is admitted, but all the other competing priorities do not go away! Whilst this is never an easy situation the support of the Traveller Education Support Service can be helpful. They can be contacted via the local authority. If a school has a tradition of admitting and teaching Gypsy and Traveller children, in some cases there may be a Traveller Support teacher or teaching assistant (O'Hanlon and Holmes 2004).

If schools set up and maintain effective relationships at the outset, this can contribute to good attendance on the part of Gypsy, Roma and Traveller children (DfES 2003b). Attendance is, however, a significant concern for pupils from a travelling background. Poor attendance will certainly have an impact on attainment and ultimately the success of these children in future life. This area is explored in the next section.

Attendance

As children approach secondary school age, concerns over racism and behaviour can impact on children's attendance and retention. Derrington (2005) explains in a study of behaviour and exclusion in secondary schools that:

although students' behaviour was perceived to be good by their primary school teachers, problems began to emerge during the first year at secondary school and twenty-four (out of 44) pupils had self-excluded by the age of 14 years. Furthermore, one in three of the students were temporarily excluded on at least one occasion (Derrington 2005: 55).

Derrington goes on to say that the number one factor, which pupils and parents state as a reason for poor attendance, is where schools do not address the problems associated with racism and name-calling. In Derrington's (2005) study, Year 6 teachers predicted many of the problems which Gypsy, Roma and Traveller children went on to experience subsequently in secondary school.

Similarly, in a study of Scottish Gypsy and Traveller families, Jordan (2001) explained that:

> the essentially excluding school system and the self-excluding Gypsy or Traveller pupil (condoned by parents) conspired to perpetuate cycles of underachievement and marginalization, confirming their social exclusion with society (Jordan 2001: 117).

Attendance is an important factor in children's achievement in school. Below are what the DfES (2003b) highlights as effective ways of supporting attendance in schools:

Activities – Towards better attendance

- Follow up non-attendance as soon as possible. This conveys the message that a pupil's presence is valued.

- Establish a high level of contact between schools and parents. Developing an effective dialogue helps parents to understand the value of education and their value in supporting the school.

- Provide training for staff on the varied circumstances which pupils face in school and how best to help them.

- Audit curriculum provision, social support, bullying and race equality practice to ensure that these are not factors in poor attendance.

Case Study – Becky's story

Loads of people bully me. It's mostly boys in my class. They say I don't wash and they call me dog or cow. They don't say it to other girls … I used to make up excuses to teachers like saying I was sick when I wasn't.

Becky, KS 3 pupil.
(Derrington 2005: 59)

Becky's response is typical of many children's – if there is a problem, don't go to school. Realistically, this is not just the response of Gypsy, Roma and Traveller children: all children regardless of background, culture or ethnicity may respond in a 'fight or flight' manner when they experience difficulties in school. In Becky's case her school has developed strategies to address some of the difficulties she had been experiencing.

> ## Case Study – Helping Becky
>
> She meets with Jenny [NQT] once a week who is interested in special needs work – we thought it'd be quite nice for Becky to have a young female mentor … she's been doing a lot of work with her looking at self-esteem, working out … 'cos the local community is not particularly tolerant of other people, of 'others' if you like, whatever the other is and she gets a lot of stick in the community and it's difficult for us to deal with it because it's happening outside school or we're talking about people's parents that have said things and it's a very sensitive issue. So Jenny's been working with her trying to help and guide her through that sort of thing and help her solve the problems on her own. Becky's mother (Derrington 2005: 59).

Note how mentors (as previously discussed in Chapter 4) can be useful in supporting children both socially and emotionally which ultimately supports attendance. As schools change and the role of teachers and other adults in the classroom changes also in response to the remodelling of the work-force and *Every Child Matters* (DfES 2006c) there are potential opportunities for a more co-ordinated approach to supporting pupils in this way. It could be a teaching assistant or someone from the Gypsy, Roma and Traveller community who takes on the role of mentor.

O'Hanlon and Holmes (2004) explain that exclusion should be used as a sanction only as a last resort. Excluding children from school only contributes to family perceptions that it is not worth going to school. They go on to explain further a selection of practical strategies for encouraging better attendance:

- Liaison with the Education Welfare Service: for instance, providing transport where families move frequently between short-stay, illegal encampments.

- Provision of effective records: to identify relevant personal information and strategies for supporting individuals, which can then be given to families to take to their next school. This action provides continuity during periods of 'interrupted' schooling.

- Distance learning materials: in some local authorities the Traveller Education Support Service has produced materials which pupils can take with them during periods of absence. Even if pupils are physically not in school the negative impact on their education can be reduced.

Gypsy, Roma and Traveller children have a right to education under domestic law. Do you know the law in respect of Gypsy, Roma and Traveller children? The following will help:

Laws affecting Gypsy, Roma and Traveller children

Parents

Education Act 1996

- All parents have a duty to ensure that their children receive efficient, full-time education.

Local Authorities

Education Act (1996)

- Local authorities have a duty to monitor attendance and take action where necessary

- Local authorities have a duty to provide suitable places for all pupils, even those resident on a temporary basis.

Race Relations (Amendment) Act 2000

From 2003, Gypsy and Roma Travellers and Travellers of Irish heritage were included in the DfES's ethnic categories. It therefore became law for all institutions including schools to monitor the implementation of this law and to take action in cases of racist bullying (O'Hanlon and Holmes 2004).

Human Rights Act 1998

This enshrines the 'right to education' and the right for parents to have their religious and philosophical convictions respected by the state.

The law requires all parents, including those in Gypsy and Traveller families, to send their children to school when they are of compulsory school age (Education Act 1996). Even during periods of interrupted schooling, parents are expected to ensure that their children attend school. Schools for their part are required to provide places for children, even when those children are in the area only for a limited period of time. The DfES has explained in detail the legal issues associated with admissions and attendance (DfES 2003b).

Anti-bullying and anti-racism

The Race Relations (Amendment) Act 2000, highlighted in Chapter 1, places great emphasis on the need to provide for good race relations, to deal with racist incidents and to report them to local authorities. Since many Gypsy, Roma and Traveller children fall within this legislation, schools have a legal responsibility to deal with the one issue which all pupils and parents reported as leading to poor attendance and violence in school – racism and associated name-calling (Derrington 2005).

Tension exists for Gypsy, Roma and Traveller families between the need for an education and the respect that is lost due to such racism, which many of their children suffer personally in school:

> Getting an education is important for everyone, but it's more important for us because we're different. We're Gypsies. If we get an education, then people will respect us and not call us 'dirty, old Gypos'. Mrs Heart, parent (Bhopal 2004: 55).

Reynolds et al. (2003) confirm that the same is true in Northern Ireland where Irish Gypsy and Traveller children were educated in separate schools until a few years ago. Whilst most of these children experienced bullying, name-calling and in some cases physical abuse due to their ethnicity, their families felt unable to approach the school concerned. For most, such experiences go a long way in confirming their attitude that it is 'not worth' going to school'. OFSTED (1996b) said in turn that many of the incidents of exclusion of Traveller children related to physical responses to racism and bullying by non-Gypsy children. Schools do find this difficult as there is a culture of 'non-reporting' of racist incidents. As one boy said:

> All the Traveller children I know have the attitude that if you are not seen to be sorting out your own problems, you are weak. You have failed. (Derrington 2005: 50)

This attitude recalls the cultural aspects of identity and masculinity discussed earlier (Levinson and Sparkes 2003). It is important that all staff in a school look at their own attitudes and also the ways in which they talk to Gypsy, Roma and Traveller pupils. Further, there is a danger that teaching staff can themselves have racist attitudes.

Activities – Avoiding racist comments in school

Read the following comments from a Head of Year in a secondary school.

Think about any comments that you or your colleagues have made which might be seen as being racist.

What can you do to avoid such comments?

> The majority of the staff welcomed them [the Travellers] with open arms, tried very hard with them. But I have to say, and I am ashamed to say it … a very small minority were terrible. As far as they were concerned, they were thieves from the minute they walked into the building, they were vagabonds and they never gave them a chance no matter how many times I took these staff to one side and said you can't. They were unprofessional. I had better not say too much really but they were totally unprofessional in their approach to it … there were certainly times when I witnessed them on a corridor perhaps disciplining them for something they wouldn't discipline another child for because of who they were. I'm ashamed to say that but I have got to tell the truth. Teacher (Derrington 2005: 60).

Bhopal et al. (2000) explain that some schools are very proactive in dealing with racism. Whether it is the headteacher, the Gypsy, Roma and Traveller Support teacher, or a class teacher, in the most effective schools everyone takes racism very seriously. They suggest the following steps to react positively to the challenges of racism:

- ■ All incidents should be recognized, formally recorded and investigated.

- ■ Victims of racism need clear, and if necessary public support.

- ■ Effective sanctions are needed to deal with racism.

- ■ School pastoral systems need to deal with racism sensitively.

As we noted in Chapter 4, racism must be taken seriously. Where racism and bullying are appropriately addressed, this can have a very positive impact on the relationship between a Gypsy, Roma and Traveller family and school. In fact, this can break the circle of distrust that can exist.

Time to reflect – Pastoral support in school

If my son has a problem, he would go straight to the Traveller teacher and the Traveller teacher would then try to sort it out. The Traveller teacher is very good and patient with my son. Sometimes I don't know what my son would do without him. He has helped my son a lot. And what they [Traveller Education Support Service] do is a good thing, because we know that there is someone there who will help us when we have a problem and see things from our side and try and understand what we say and what we are thinking. Mother (Bhopal 2004: 56).

Another secondary school has the following clear sequence in place for responding to bullying (Bhopal et al. 2000):

- Record the incident on a referral form.

- Inform colleagues, particularly if the incident arose out of a situation where everyone should be more vigilant (for example unsupervized toilets).

- Where necessary, tell both sets of parents that the incident is being dealt with.

Jordan (2001) highlights the government's deficiencies in respect of dealing with bullying and racism of Gypsy, Roma and Traveller children. There have been significant developments in legislation and the media has given much attention to this area as a result (for instance, in the case of the Stephen Lawrence Inquiry as we noted earlier in Chapter 4). However, Jordan (2001) points out that there is no mention of Gypsies and Travellers in Scottish legislative developments on housing and social inclusion. Although governmental rhetoric on racism and bullying does not always extend to Gypsy, Roma and Traveller children, you have to start somewhere in addressing the problem. As Reynolds et al. (2003) have said, bullying and racism should not be left to a third party because these are things you do not want to get involved in. If everyone acts to develop an inclusive school and responds constructively to racism and bullying, we will have gone a long way in dispelling some of the reasons for parental lack of faith in schools.

Developing an inclusive approach to different cultures can help to root out some of the negative attitudes which children and families have for people 'who are different'. The displays, topics and content of lessons all have a part to play in developing an inclusive ethos in schools. The overt and hidden curriculum are both important in this respect.

The curriculum

Whilst the overt curriculum (QCA 1999) includes the various levels of planned activities which children experience in school, the hidden curriculum includes all those elements of a school which communicate the school's view of itself and others. Displays are a very good example of this. One parent explained the importance of positive images of Gypsy, Roma and Traveller children:

Case Study – Inclusion in the hidden curriculum

There are some boards with pictures of Travellers, the Traveller Teacher has lots of photos and books in her room. The children made a calendar about our life as well. The school does more than any other school. They've always had Travellers here and know us and do what they can to make sure that we feel included like everyone else is. The Traveller teacher and the Head are always eager to find out about us and learn about our ways. So, this makes us feel welcome and that they care. Mrs. Lock, parent (Bhopal 2004: 56).

Bhopal does, however, go on to say that Gypsies, Roma and Travellers are rarely seen in school textbooks. There are a few notable exceptions. One of these is *The Travelling People* by Wormington et al. (2003). The important point here is that this type of book should be made available to all children, not just those most directly touched by Gypsy, Roma and Traveller communities. How could you incorporate this information book in school? The main contents of the book are outlined in the following table.

The Traveller People

- Contents.
- The Travelling people (introduction).
- Time line (a history of Travellers in Britain).
- Travelling People in Great Britain and Ireland (an overview of groups and terms).
- Gypsy and Roma fact file.
- Irish, Scottish and Welsh fact file.
- New Traveller and Bargee fact file.
- Upper or lower case (terms for different groups).
- Customs and traditions.
- Circus fact file.
- Showmen and Fairground people fact file.
- Where Travellers live.
- Occupations.
- Glossary and bibliography.

(Wormington et al. 2003)

According to one of the Gypsy, Roma and Traveller mothers cited earlier, it gave her pleasure to know that her children and indeed the whole class were working together on a topic about her community. This promotes inclusion through the choice of topic in the curriculum. In primary school, cross-curricular topics in history and geography especially make the development of English skills meaningful when they are combined with a focus on the Gypsy, Roma and Traveller community.

The oral tradition of many Gypsy, Roma and Traveller groups also lends itself to a focus on storytelling. Many stories in Gypsy, Roma and Traveller cultures are handed down through the generations as spoken forms whch have never been written down. In fact this is the origin of most of the traditional tales which are central to our culture. *Little Red Riding Hood* originates from Italy, but was told to Charles Perrault in the South of France during the seventeenth century. Only the interest of Louis the XIV and his court led to the writing down of these tales. Once in print, there is a tendency for tales to be changed according to the teller of the tale (Zipes 1976).

Gypsy, Roma and Traveller tales have much to offer schools in the development of greater understanding of other cultures. Combined with the use of drama, storytelling has much to offer the teacher. It has the dual effective of enlivening the lesson, whilst giving a positive message that tales from all cultures are valued, including those from Gypsy, Roma and Traveller cultures. This can be used to good effect to develop a unit of work in primary schools as follows:

Activities – English unit on Gypsy folk tales

- Use the book *Gypsy Folk Tales* edited by Amabel Williams-Ellis (1973).

- Tell one of the stories from the book.

- Remember, in storytelling it's important to know the main points and signposts in the story. You don't have to retell the story word for word.

- Children can use props to act out key events in the story.

- Read a version and annotate the key features and language on an interactive whiteboard.

- Model to the children your own version of the story.

- Invite alternative characters, settings and storylines from the children using the story, which you then scribe.

- Children can develop a sequel to the story, which they plan and write up during an extended writing session.

- At the end of the unit ask some of the children to read out their stories and others to 'tell' their story without reading.

- Can the children recognize the difference in language between the written and oral forms? This reinforces understanding about the difference between written and spoken forms, dialect and accent: all features of language variation (QCA 1999).

- Can the children recognize words from Gypsy, Roma and Traveller languages and dialects?

- Make a display of the stories and the new words children have learned.

Inclusion of culturally sensitive topics is equally possible in secondary schools. Cross-curricular English activities can be used to develop interesting and purposeful activities between different subjects. Can you think of any other possibilities?

Activities – Cross-curricular opportunities in secondary schools

English	Links to other subjects
Write a report on different dwellings of different peoples.	Geography
Make a time line of a Roma Gypsy from the early 1900s in Eastern Europe to their arrival in England in the 1990s.	History
Make an Irish tale booklet illustrated with Celtic artwork.	Art
Devize a leaflet to advertise the ancient Statutes Fair on behalf of a visiting Showground family.	Business and vocational subjects

It is important to recognize that all children will benefit from activities such as these. In the previous chapter, for instance, you will have been introduced to the difficulties that Black children can face in school. There is evidence that strategies explained in this chapter can be effective in supporting children from minority ethnic communities other than that of Gypsies, Roma and Travellers. Not only will these activities contribute to the development of skills and understanding in English, but they will contribute to the wider understanding of other cultures which is enshrined in the Race Relations (Amendment) Act 2000. By developing an inclusive curriculum, using inclusive materials and teaching methods which promote inclusion, teachers and schools are more likely to avoid some of the poor behaviour and violence which have been explored above. There are some important steps beyond the curriculum which teachers can take in order to encourage positive classroom behaviour and school discipline in Gypsy, Roma and Traveller children.

Behaviour, communication and the peer group

You saw in the preceding sections that masculinity was often reinforced by prowess of a physical nature and that Gypsy, Roma and Traveller boys especially can react unpredictably to name-calling, being quick to resort to violence (Levinson and Sparkes 2003). Similarly, in the previous chapter we discussed the issues of masculinity with reference to 'Black boys'. One teacher summarizes this as follows:

Case Study – One teacher's view of behaviour

I probably shouldn't say this, but they're charming one moment, little devils the next. It's a powder keg, and quite often you know they're playing the system. They know just how far they can go. You wouldn't believe the number of fights some of the boys get involved in, among themselves as well as with other boys, yet somehow it's never their fault. Erica, Secondary teacher (Levinson and Sparkes 2003: 593).

As teachers we should be careful not to generalize based on the reports of a single teacher. However, Derrington (2005) offers an explanation for some of the perceptions held by secondary school teachers, based on the predictions of Year 6 primary school teachers of Gypsy, Roma and Traveller pupils. In addition to the problems of attendance and the lack of a central, trusted adult, Derrington points to the following factors relating to behaviour:

- Hostile exchanges between pupils and teachers as a result of a teacher's arbitrary, hostile or aggressive manner, provoking a pupil to react in a volatile way.

- Direct communication style of pupils misinterpreted by teachers as a sign of disrespect.

- Social and academic grouping of Gypsy, Roma and Traveller children with other children in lower ability groups, whereby other pupils may have low social skills and their own behavioural issues, providing the potential for conflict.

- Peer group approval resulting in 'acting out' behaviours. Alternatively, Gypsy, Roma and Traveller pupils try to establish themselves in the 'pecking order' of the peer group through fighting with others.

Parents of Gypsy, Roma and Traveller pupils often sided with their children when they perceived that the teacher had been aggressive in speaking to them. One mother states:

They [teachers] don't know how to speak to Gypsy children. They shout and tell them what to do but they don't like to be bossed. They don't like to be ordered. If they ask them nicely it's a different thing but if they tell them and boss them they're wasting their time (Derrington 2005: 57).

The direct and open style of communication adopted by some Gypsy, Roma and Traveller pupils is sometimes seen as a very adult quality which can be admired by teachers (Derrington 2005). Others, however, see this as being overly familiar. When looked at in the context of the close-knit nature of Gypsy, Roma and Traveller families and the assumption that these children will take on responsibilities from an early age, then it is easy to see why Gypsy, Roma and Traveller children communicate at such an adult level. Put yourself in their place:

Activities – Talking to Gypsies, Roma and Travellers

Which of these topics would you feel comfortable talking about?

- The football match last weekend.

- The last episode of your favourite soap opera.

- Your holiday from last summer.

- Your first name.

- Your age.

- What you think of some other pupils in the same year.

- Why you have decided to teach a particular lesson.

Some teachers may be comfortable with any of the above topics. Others may recoil at all of these. The important point here is the way a teacher is able to steer pupils away from topics without using an aggressive tone.

As we saw earlier in Chapter 2, knowing two or more languages is an advantage in academic learning. Some Gypsy, Roma and Traveller families speak languages other than English. Not all Gypsies, for instance, speak Romani but most understand some of its words (O'Hanlon and Holmes 2004). Words like *gorja* (a term used for a non-Gypsy) are sometimes used as a riposte to those pupils who call Gypsy children names. O'Hanlon and Holmes (2004) outline a case study in which they encouraged the use of some home language as part of an inclusive approach to Gypsy, Roma and Traveller children:

Activities – Promoting the use of a home language in school

- Raise awareness of commonly used words, which may arise in the classroom situation.

- Explore connections between the home language and English.

- Challenge views that Gypsies, Roma and Travellers are deficient in the use of language: they use language *differently* but not necessarily *deficiently*.

- Dual-language books can be useful, but some parents can be dismissive of 'showing their children up' by using books with home language words in.

Whilst a celebration of the range of languages in a school can help the development of an inclusive whole-school ethos, consistency in the application of a rewards and sanctions system is also very important. Bhopal et al. (2000) summarize the features of an effective school in respect of behaviour:

- They provide a public framework for good behaviour, which is explained carefully to parents and children. For example, in many of these schools the pupil Code of Conduct is displayed in public places throughout the school.

- All staff in the school apply the framework consistently.

- The headteacher has a very important role in setting the tone of relations with both Gypsy, Roma and Traveller pupils and parents. This should be welcoming and supportive. Leadership comes from the headteacher and the school's governing body in this respect.

Any school framework for rewards and sanctions must be applied sensitively. Derrington (2005) explains that teachers should be careful in their expectations for Traveller children in respect of homework. Many Gypsy, Roma and Traveller children have difficulty in finding the space to complete homework. Sometimes parents themselves have poor basic skills and are, therefore, not able to help their children in the same way that some others do. So when a Gypsy or Traveller pupil fails to complete homework on time, it would be wrong to immediately issue a detention in a secondary school, if this is the normal procedure. Where secondary schools encourage dialogue with Gypsy, Roma and Traveller parents this can help to explain and justify school policy on things like uniform and the wearing of jewellery.

Consistency in policy and practice throughout the school is vitally important. Derrington (2005) explains the case of Peter who was excluded for retaliating when another pupil called him names. The other boy was not excluded. Shortly after this incident Peter opted out of school – he was only 12.

Time to reflect

◆ Have you examined your own beliefs and knowledge about Traveller, Roma and Gypsy communities?

◆ Has your school developed a positive and welcoming ethos towards Traveller, Roma and Gypsy families?

◆ Does your school have a consistent policy in place to deal with racism, name-calling and bullying?

◆ Has your school made constructive links with the Traveller Education Support Service?

◆ Is your curriculum and teaching style relevant and supportive of Gypsy, Roma and Traveller children?

◆ Do you monitor the achievement of Gypsy, Roma and Traveller pupils, setting high expectations for all your pupils?

◆ Are families closely involved in your school to ensure good behaviour and learning in a happy and safe environment?

Reflection and review

- Gypsy, Roma and Traveller communities are varied in make-up and background.

- Look at the diagram below. Ultimately, the success of Gypsy, Roma and Traveller pupils in school is built on the trust that has been developed from the first contact between a family and the school.

- With appropriate support and by maintaining good communication with families, schools are able to help pupils achieve and maintain good attendance, even if their stay at a school is only temporary.

- Gypsy, Roma and Traveller children should no more be subject to 'extreme racism, discimination and stereotyping greater than any other minority ethnic group' (DES 1985).

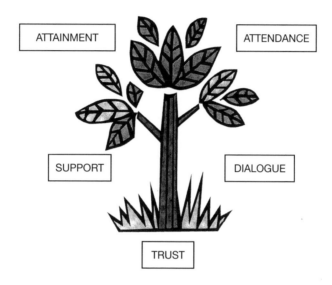

Key Points

- There is no one approach or method of working with Gypsy, Roma and Traveller children which is guaranteed to work, as is the case in many areas of education.

- Try to avoid the stereotypes which are sometimes associated with Gypsy, Roma and Travellers. One of these is that Gypsy, Roma and Traveller parents are not interested in their children's education.

- Learning alongside older brothers, cousins and especially their fathers not only allows boys to develop practical skills, but is very important also in helping them to establish their masculinity.

- The close family relationships of Gypsy, Roma and Traveller children should be considered when admitting very young children to school.

- As children approach secondary school age, concerns over racism and behaviour can impact on their attendance and retention.

We look next in Chapter 6, at an issue which has emerged throughout our discussions, the importance of working with parents and the local community.

Working with parents and the local community

This chapter looks at:

■ the need for parental involvement

■ why minority ethnic parents do not get involved in their child's education

■ building relationships with minority ethnic parents

■ defining and exploring types of parental involvement

■ how to get more minority ethnic parents involved in their child's education

■ approaches to working with the local community.

So far we have discussed different learner groups in relative isolation from one another. One of the key issues which links these learner groups together relates to the importance of working effectively with parents and the local community to improve the quality of educational provision and raise children's attainment. This has been well documented over many years (DfES 2003a; Smit et al. 2002), and continues to be an important issue for all practitioners to consider, whether they are training, newly qualified or experienced. Key questions frequently asked by practitioners include:

■ How can I foster strong and effective connections with the parents of the children I teach?

■ What strategies are available for me to nurture parental involvement and partnerships?

■ Which professional groups and outside agencies can I work with to support practice in the classroom and in my own setting?

In this chapter we provide information about the practices of some of the most successful groups who work with minority ethnic parents, specifically those from Asylum Seeker/Refugee and Gypsy, Roma and Traveller communities. Whilst the importance of the local community is recognized, the majority of this chapter will focus on the involvement of parents in strengthening and extending learning experiences and thus helping to raise academic achievement throughout the age phases.

The need for parental involvement

It is important to initially recognize and appreciate the many arguments which have been presented by educationalists, including Shah (2001) and Munn (1993), with regard to why parents should be involved in their children's education. They would argue:

- Parental involvement improves children's educational performance.

- Parents are already involved as the primary educators of their children before they enter the education system.

- Parental involvement extends the contexts for learning.

- Parental involvement enhances children's self-esteem.

- Parental involvement improves parent–child relationships.

- Parental involvement helps parents to develop positive attitudes towards settings and a better understanding of the schooling process.

With such persuasive reasoning it is not surprising that a number of studies of exemplary practice across the age phases identify parental involvement as one of the key variables associated with a setting's effectiveness in general and with pupil attainment (Chaboudy et al. 2001 cited in Fitzgerald, 2004). Whilst it has been argued that many parents do not see themselves as 'educators', they will support their children's intellectual and social development irrespective of a family's social, economic, religious or cultural background (Miller et al. 2005). However, from the growing body of research into home-setting relations, we know that those parents who find it most difficult to be involved in a relationship with their child's school and to act on their child's behalf are minority ethnic parents (Crozier 2001). For an interesting discussion into the arguments for more parental involvement in supporting the social and educational achievements of children please take a look at:

Driessen et al. (2005) and you are recommended to refer particularly to pages 514 and 515.

Why minority ethnic parents do not get involved in their child's education

One prevailing viewpoint amongst practitioners today is that parents from minority ethnic groups are 'hard to reach' or 'uninvolved' in their children's education (Cork 2005). It is important, however, for us to consider whether this view is based solely on academic research or on pre-conceived personal perceptions. The activity overleaf is designed to help you explore and reflect on a range of different reasons as to why minority ethnic parents may appear to not be involved in their child's education.

Activities – 'Are they just "*uninterested*" in their children's education?'

Take a moment to read and reflect on the reasoning identified below, considering why minority ethnic parents, particularly those of asylum seeker/refugee and Gypsy, Roma/Traveller backgrounds, may not actively get involved in their children's education. Please tick the reasons you believe to be applicable, making a note of any others you know of using the spaces provided.

☐ Lack of time.

☐ Lack of energy.

☐ Busy lives outside of the setting.

☐ Work commitments – long hours, irregular shift patterns.

☐ Family commitments – younger children needing to be looked after.

☐ Lack of a shared language – English as an additional language or no English language.

☐ Visits to the setting are perceived to be an uncomfortable experience – own education proved to be a difficult time.

☐ Lack of own education – poor literacy, oral or numeracy skills.

☐ Burdened with social difficulties – poverty, poor housing.

☐ Parents' fear and suspicion of the practitioner(s).

☐ Geographical issues – difficulties with mobility or access.

☐ Cultural, class or religious reasoning.

■ _____

■ _____

■ _____

Select any three of the reasons you have identified above and consider possible practical strategies you could put into place to overcome these potential issues.

Discuss your ideas with colleagues or your headteacher.

There are many other factors and reasons as to why minority ethnic parents do not get involved in their child's education. Those interested in this topic are encouraged to read the research of Wright et al. (2000) and Gillborn and Youdell (2000, cited in Crozier 2001: 329).

It is important to note that all schools across the country, irrespective of whether or not they have minority ethnic children, now face a greater challenge in encouraging parental involvement due to the need for CRB (Criminal Records Bureau) checks to be conducted on those wishing to work with children or other vulnerable members of society. Whilst these are designed to protect youngsters, parents may perceive the complicated paperwork, designated fees and lengthy amount of time required to process the application as an unnecessary burden to work with children for one afternoon per week. (Details and guidelines relating to these CRB checks can be found on www.crb.gov.uk).

Building relationships with minority ethnic parents

By engaging with the previous activity it is likely that you may have identified *'Parents' fear and suspicion of the practitioner(s)'* as one of the contributing factors towards a lack of involvement from minority ethnic parents. To successfully work with these parents, particularly those from asylum seeker/refugee and Gypsy, Roma and Traveller backgrounds, a trusting, warm and supportive relationship must be forged and sustained. It is important to recognize that this kind of relationship will not suddenly develop – it may take practitioners a number of years to successfully establish a relationship of this quality (Macbeth 1989, OECD 1997, Stacey 1991).

If educational settings are truly committed to supporting these parents, they need to plan carefully exactly *how* these relationships will be positively developed and effectively sustained. A number of schools have built and maintained relationships, particularly with Gypsy, Roma and Traveller parents, through the liaison role of minority ethnic groups including the Traveller Education Service (TES) (DfES 2003b). In both a Primary and Secondary setting in the North East of England, a senior practitioner is the designated named person who is responsible for developing a close relationship with local Gypsy, Roma and Traveller families. By providing easy access to sympathetic help and advice on a range of matters, practitioners are able to build mutual trust and respect between parents and the school, developing a strong reputation based on positive action and support. This approach is transferable and applicable to *all* parents, irrespective of whether or not they come from minority ethnic backgrounds (Reay 1998).

Implications for future practice

To build and sustain effective relationships with parents, practitioners need to:

- Give time to those parents who need it – this may be before and/or after the setting opens/closes or even during teaching time.

- Offer support and advice as and when they can, not only relating to educational issues but also to personal, social and health concerns.

- Be sympathetic to their needs.

- Work to build trust – if they say they intend to do something they must follow it through and complete it to the best of their ability (Adapted from Miller et al. 2005).

To successfully implement these strategies a large number of interpersonal and professional skills need to be effectively utilized, along with a very good understanding of the following:

- pupils' language

- pupils'learning needs

- pupils' ethnic/religious backgrounds

- pupils' immigration status.

This can only be developed if the setting is resolutely committed to ensuring a shared responsibility for the integration of all pupils and their parents into the community. For schools to successfully develop and sustain these relationships the following must be in place:

- An explicit, whole-school culture of respect, care and safety.

- Strong leadership from a committed headteacher, supported by a dedicated senior management team.

- A positive and welcoming attitude on the part of all of the staff in the school setting.

- A well-formulated policy of practice which is regularly reviewed.

- Regular in-service training for all staff, both teaching and non-teaching, on current issues and developments on the education of minority ethnic children. (DfES 2003a)

Whilst few issues enjoy such universal support as the idea that parental and community involvement are essential for successful schooling and children's learning, it is important to have a clear understanding of what is meant by the term 'parental involvement'.

Defining parental involvement

Whilst the term 'parental involvement' is frequently referred to in policy and professional practice, very few definitions are explicit with regard to what it actually means. A number of researchers including Vincent et al (2003), Tomlinson (1991) and Epstein (1990) have identified various types of parental involvement ranging from repairing library books or helping out on trips, to parent-aides working in the classroom or giving home-based support with reading.

Most school settings will have developed enough to be able to implement specific policies to formulate a common understanding on parental involvement and to encourage parents to be fully involved in the education of their children. The activity opposite is designed to encourage you to reflect on your practice to date.

Activities – What do we already do?

Using the chart below, list ways in which you promote the involvement of parents in your classroom and how the educational setting as a whole attempts to promote this involvement. Set yourself a time limit of *five* minutes to undertake this activity – which strategies immediately come to mind?

My classroom	The setting

Take a few moments to compare your lists to the details presented in a) your policy relating to parental involvement and b) in light of the discussion made earlier in this chapter. Reflect on the lists as you engage with the remainder of this chapter, considering how you could adapt current practice and/or introduce new strategies to promote working with parents and the local community.

This activity could also be used and adapted to support a whole-school staff development and discussion on this topic.

Exploring types of parental involvement

As previously mentioned there are many different types of parental involvement (Pugh and De'Ath 1989). For the purposes of this chapter we will examine in turn the types supported by research undertaken by Epstein (2001, cited in Driessen et al. 2005):

- Involvement of parents of children under 5.

- Involvement in learning processes at home or in the setting.

- Involvement in supporting the school or setting.

- Involvement in governing the school or setting.

- Home-setting relations.

Involvement of parents of children under 5

Bridge (2001) acknowledges the importance of working with parents in the early years as they are in a prime position to observe, monitor and evaluate their children's development. Over the years they build up an in-depth knowledge of their children which can, if accessed by the school, add a great deal to practitioners' understanding. By working collaboratively, a number of advantages present themselves for consideration:

- Parents have an expertise in commenting on their child's development.

- Parents' intimate knowledge of their children can be described by them.

- Parental knowledge can complement professional information.

- The information can highlight differing behaviours in different settings.

- The information can serve to highlight concerns regarding progress.

- Parents can provide a realistic appraisal of their children.

It is important for practitioners to remember that, irrespective of the age of the child, the points identified above can support those working in the Primary or Secondary age phase. The activity below is designed to make you consider the importance and value of collecting and using parental information on children to support learning and teaching in the classroom.

Time to reflect – Parental knowledge

- Do *you* or the school seek information from parents about their children?

- *When* do you collect this information?

- *What* information do you collect from the parents?

- *How* do you collect this information?

- Do you *review* and *update* this information? *When* do you undertake this review? Do you review this information *with* the parents?

It is important to remember, however, that a number of pupils from asylum seeker/refugee and Gypsy, Roma and Traveller communities who are currently in settings across the country may not have had the opportunity to attend any form of pre-setting or Early Years setting, including Children's Centres. Any child without pre-school experience may already be at risk of under-achievement (DfES 2003a).

To support parents with young children, Fitzgerald (2004) describes how a number of Traveller Education Support Services have devized Play Boxes and Play Sacks, all focused on the six areas of learning in the Early Years Foundation Stage, which are for loaning to parents. Staff who have been trained in using the resources, which contain high quality learning materials, are able to share the training with parents, who in turn then use the resources with their young children at home. Educational settings can then capitalize on these early experiences at home, in their links with parents and their work with the youngest children.

Activities – Constructing a play box/sack

Select *one* of the following areas of learning below:

■ *Mathematical* development.

■ *Creative* development.

■ *Physical* development.

With reference to the Stepping Stones and Early Learning Goals detailed in the *Curriculum Guidance for the Foundation Stage* (DfES 1999), consider what you would put in a play box or a play sack which would support and develop knowledge, skills and understanding relating to the selected area of learning.

Consider the importance of selecting materials which are not gender biased and positively promote and represent different cultures and communities. Reflect on possible materials which could be used with older pupils who may still be accessing parts of the Curriculum Guidance due to learning needs.

The activity above highlights how simple it is to use resources readily found in Early Years settings to produce an effective learning aid which can encourage involvement and support parents in working with their children at home on meaningful and educational activities. There is a wealth of additional strategies available to Early Years practitioners to ensure parents are involved in their children's education. These include:

■ Making home visits.

■ Providing community mother and toddler groups.

■ Providing book, toy and game libraries.

■ Providing parent/child/practitioner informal meetings.

■ Encouraging parents to come in as helpers.

- Providing open day sessions/induction days for parents and children.

- Allowing parents to contribute to the records kept on their children.

- Providing home-setting notebooks.

- Loaning out videos which show practice in the setting.

- Keeping the parents up to date with developments through notices, letters, messages, conversations, meetings, posters and pamphlets.

- Providing interpreters and translators during parent–practitioner meetings.

- Engaging parents with early intervention programmes (OFSTED 1999b).

The activity below examines this final point above relating to early intervention programmes.

Activities – Early intervention programmes

A wide number of early intervention programmes are available for practitioners and parents to adopt and engage with in the early years, both on a local and national level (SureStart, for example). All of these support the idea that when parents are centrally involved in programmes, children can make cognitive gains which are sustained over time.

Programmes which place high importance on involving parents directly in activities fostering the child's development are likely to have a positive impact on the abilities of the child, but the earlier they are started and the longer they continue the greater the benefit to the child.

Talk with your Early Years Co-ordinator in your setting or with colleagues in your LA about any projects which focus on play, language development and/or comprehension. Consider which programmes are used by the setting or which could be adapted to support and extend current practice.

Involvement in learning processes at home or in an educational setting

A range of effective strategies can be used by practitioners to build parental involvement in learning processes at home or in an educational setting, for example Children's Centres (DfES 2006b). The best known example of this is home reading, where parents are encouraged to hear their children read regularly at home. Practitioners, however, need to ensure that parents are well supported by way of providing a range of simple, practical strategies to help them successfully undertake this work at home. This could be achieved through:

- A simple list of supportive guidance to aid the reading process.

- A pamphlet produced by the setting, using pictures and text in both English and the mother tongue.

- Practitioners talking about and modelling the process of home reading to parents during a timetabled session in the school day.

- Workshops being run before or after sessions to support parents.

- Video packs produced by the setting to support parents at home.

It is important for practitioners to carefully select strategies which are appropriate for the parents to use as they may have poor literacy skills. A primary setting in North London has introduced a reading project which involves parents receiving explicit training and payments for working with Years 1 and 2 children whose reading skills are in need of development. The success of this project is evident in the rise in reading attainment and in the skills of the parents who have a better understanding of the setting's way of teaching (see www.standards.gov.uk/parental involvement/does/multi_ethnic.doc).

Whilst literacy is very important, so is the development of both children's and parents' numeracy skills, as the case study below shows:

Case Study 'Keeping up with the children' – Family numeracy

An exciting example of good practice relates to the work of the Traveller Education Project (TEP) and the Hertfordshire Numeracy Team. Collaborating with three local primary settings, numeracy training was delivered to Traveller parents over three afternoon sessions.

Whilst initially being informed about the former National Numeracy Strategy (NNS) and its implications for their children, parents were allowed to watch a three-part lesson delivered by a member of staff. Parents were then given the opportunity to discuss new maths strategies with the practitioner whilst exploring activities they could use with their children at home.

All of the parents were given a maths pack full of educational resources which they could take away with them, along with a booklet detailing suggested activities. Whilst currently working on a video for parents which demonstrates ways of using the pack, the TEP are preparing similar training linked to the latest National Strategy developments (see www.thegrid.org. uk/learning/mecss/centres/traveller/good_practice.html).

There are many other agencies and support groups to assist in this kind of work. The Basic Skills Agency, for example, delivers a range of activities and projects specifically for adults in relation to literacy, numeracy and the use of ICT, in an attempt to raise adults' achievements as well as giving parents that extra confidence to support their children who are engaged in home-based activities.

When planning successful home activities, practitioners need to consider the culturally defined roles of the father and mother figures in the family, the family lifestyle and cultural background. Some activities can be adapted to almost any home situation and undertaken on a day-to-day basis. Practitioners can encourage parents and children to undertake these activities together whilst focusing particularly on the opportunities that the activities provide for learning. These include:

- Television viewing – this is a pastime for adults and children but many rarely watch together. Practitioners can suggest appropriate programmes and send home questions in English and the mother tongue for families to discuss. This discussion can be carried over into class.

- Undertaking and talking about everyday activities or family business – for example, preparing a meal or grocery shopping.

- Talking about the setting – practitioners can encourage parents to set aside a little time to sit with their children and talk about school. Notes on what they have been doing are helpful as a support and an *aide mémoire* for the child!

- Reading – children can read to their parents and parents can read to their children. For those families with few books, book libraries are a useful community resource.

For home activities to be beneficial they need to be interesting and meaningful – not trivial tasks which parents and children have to 'get through', particularly those of a worksheet nature. Materials being sent home should be printed in different formats, having been translated into the languages spoken in the local community. Miller et al. (2005) recommend the use of face-to-face contact and exchange as a means of backing up written information, particularly as this encourages parents to ask their own questions.

Practitioners need, however, to guard against the danger of an unclear distinction of roles, with practitioners expecting parents to 'teach' at home. Practitioners and parents need to understand that their roles are different, and that their respective activities with children should be different. Practice relating to this differs from setting to setting. Rutter et al. (1998) describe how a mixed Secondary setting in North London plans homework activities which allow the children to use their refugee experiences to support them. In comparison, a Secondary setting in a Suffolk LA uses scientific homework activities which are incorporated by the practitioner, into the main teaching so that parents feel that their contributions are being valued and are supporting effective learning and teaching.

Implications for future practice

- Be explicitly clear about the roles you wish parents to play at home.

- Ensure activities take into consideration lifestyles and cultural differences.

- Avoid laborious worksheet activities – try to engage parents and children in activities which are interactive, fun and interesting.

Involvement in supporting the setting

Educational settings and the practitioners who work in them are able to adopt and implement a wide range of activities which can either directly or indirectly involve parents working with their own and other children. These include:

- Parent Practitioner Association (PPA) or Parent Friend Association (PFA) fund raising – fairs or fêtes, prize draws, jumble sales.

- Direct assistance – repairs to apparatus, toys, books, the construction of apparatus, help in the library.

- Child supervision – trips, visits, parent-aides, breakfast and homework clubs.

- Parents as tutors – working with small groups, listening to children read, playing games.

- Parents as resource practitioners – talking to groups about their own talents and experiences, for example fishing; singing; baking; language clubs for parents, practitioners and children; acting as translators and interpreters.

- Social or cultural events – assemblies, festivals, open days (Adapted from Beveridge 2005).

These activities can be adapted so that they offer a non-threatening way for parents to be involved if they do not feel comfortable or confident working with their own children and others in the classroom. OFSTED (2003) identifies the value of having a designated parents' room which offers parents a warm and undisturbed environment in which they are able to chat informally with other parents and undertake activities set by practitioners in the setting which might include creating story sacks, making new digit cards for numeracy activities, cataloguing books for the library or laminating and cutting out activity cards. This room should be available for parents to access at any time throughout the day. However, even though there are a number of strategies available, this does not necessarily mean that you will have a significant number of parents supporting these activities.

Some of the most successful settings have been able to increase the number of parents participating in activities in the setting by adopting and consistently using a range of simple yet effective strategies:

- Ensuring the welcome at Early Years level is as warm as the welcome into Secondary level, to forge a positive, long-term relationship.

- Developing positive contacts such as celebrating seasonal and religious festivals.

- Sharing traditional customs.

- Offering flexibility in the timing of meetings and interviews.

- Translating formal communications, including newsletters, into community languages where possible.

- Displaying material and directional signs around the setting in community languages and pictorial form.

- Providing interpreting facilities where possible (DfES 1999).

By making schools open and welcoming right from the onset, parents can feel comfortable and at ease and are therefore more willing to approach and support the setting.

It is, however, very important for practitioners to acknowledge that parents can bring to the setting many talents and areas of expertise which can be utilized productively to support and extend the variety of learning opportunities offered to children. Rather than settings 'training' parents to do what they require, practitioners should work to use the knowledge, skills and understanding of parents who are willing to share these with children. Children from one inner-city Primary setting in Derby, where we have undertaken some voluntary teaching work, were fortunate enough to develop skills linked to storytelling, building bird tables, making pots, erecting tents, learning cultural dances and growing vegetables, all due to the time and support given by parents. In a secondary setting in the Midlands, minority ethnic parents were encouraged to share cultural songs with Key Stage 3 children as part of a musical project on diversity. The children were taught these songs and were then allowed to work collaboratively with the parents to compose a musical score, with cultural musical instruments as an accompaniment.

Activities – Parents as a source of information

In one Infant setting in Nottingham, practitioners have found it helpful to work together with parents to produce and develop their own educational materials in terms of long-term, medium- and short-term planning. For example, such topics as *Where we live, Homes, Shops, Games we play, Where people work, Food we eat, Where we meet,* have all been developed via a collaborative effort with parents to encompass the diverse cultures of the local neighbourhood and promote positive images of people from different cultures and communities, thus helping to break down prejudice and stereotyping.

Select a future topic or unit of work you will be undertaking with your children. Consider which parents would be able to support learning and teaching in the topic or unit, reflecting on the knowledge, skills and attitudes they may be able to develop in your children. Plan for their use – how will they have a positive impact on the quality of the work planned?

Macauley (2000) describes how assemblies have been used by one setting as a way of promoting the involvement of parents. During the Spring term the main focus of the assemblies centred on the lives and contributions of great men and women. Parents from asylum seeker and refugee and Gypsy, Roma and Traveller communities were encouraged to share their views and ideas, celebrating their own heroes and heroines.

One important issue which we must consider relates to how settings can find out what skills and connections parents have. Many parents may not recognize their skills or contacts as being particularly valuable to the setting. The case study below details how one Primary setting managed to achieve this.

Case Study – Skills bank

Pioneered by Cubbington Church of England Primary School in Warwickshire, staff members developed a skills bank in the form of a questionnaire which asked parents to register any talents and contacts they had. Maiden (2006: 10) describes how parents offered more than 60 different skills, including website design and choreography, which were used throughout the setting. By asking the established network of parents to offer only one hour per term, the setting found parents were more than willing to give more of their time and this helped to reduce the need to buy in many professional services.

Further strategies and examples of good practice are provided below for you to reflect on:

- ■ Use parents to support the planning and delivery of:

    – individual lessons;

– sequences of lessons (formulation of medium-term plans);

– thematic weeks (cultural diversity, for example);

– long-term personal schemes of work (PSHE work).

■ Allow parents to come and work with individuals, pairs, small groups and the whole class, supporting learning and teaching for short or long periods of time.

■ Utilize the skills of parents by getting them to act as multilingual teaching assistants, translating and supporting children with their work.

■ Encourage parents to support practitioners in selecting multilingual and multicultural resources to support taught delivery of core and Foundation subjects.

Another important way in which parents can be more involved in settings is through becoming part of the setting's governing body.

Involvement in governing the setting

In the publication *Aiming High: Raising the Achievement of Gypsy and Traveller Pupils*, the DfES (2003b: 6) notes how recruiting and supporting Gypsy/Traveller parents as governors is acknowledged as a positive and imaginative strategy in developing the life of the setting. Many settings, however, find difficulty in attracting parents from minority ethnic backgrounds onto the governing body. Schools need to closely monitor participation rates to ensure that communities are represented and are contributing to the development of children in the setting. Involvement can be encouraged through the use of the following strategies:

■ Talking to parents about their roles and responsibilities.

■ Supporting parents in their roles and responsibilities.

■ Using a 'buddy' system which allows parents to work together with other members of their culture/community.

■ Allowing parents to attend and observe meetings so that they are aware of procedures and current issues.

■ Maintaining regular, positive contact with parents and the governing body through letters, conversations, messages and meetings. (DfES 2003b)

Whilst many parents may be apprehensive about signing themselves up for a potential four-year commitment, there are a number of short-term strategies available which are designed specifically to build home-setting relations.

Home-setting relations

This is perhaps the most fundamental area of parental involvement, particularly as home and family play a key role in children's development. With a positive relationship there will be an effective flow of information in both directions, and parental involvement projects will have a good level of success (Long, 1986). A wide range of methods can help to promote effective information exchange as discussed and adapted by Hughes (2002: 117):

- Home contracts – visits, phone calls, letters.

- Setting contracts – open days, individual parent–practitioner meetings, parents' meetings.

- Parent survey/questionnaire – to determine areas of concern, and problems, or to evaluate home-setting relations.

- Written communication – posters, calendars of events, class newsletters, setting handbooks, news boards.

- Parent handbook – basic information, contacts, suggested home activities.

- Media announcements – local press, local radio, posters and pamphlets.

- Parents' room/library.

Practitioners need to ensure that they have in place effective ways to share information with minority ethnic parents with regard to the academic progress that their children are making. Whether or not a child is achieving well or is under-achieving, minority ethnic parents need to know what is expected of their child and how they can help and support them. This can be achieved by using any of the following strategies:

- Have regular, short meetings with parents either before or after school.

- Produce comprehensive leaflets and guidance materials written in different languages relating to the National Curriculum and attainment targets.

- Hold open afternoons/evenings to allow parents to come into the setting to talk with staff members about progress, attainment and targets.

- Produce pamphlets offering simple ways to support a child at home, ensuring strategies work towards those targets a child is working on at school.

- Be available to answer any questions parents may have about their child's progress.

It is also possible to promote good relations between parents and practitioners through outings, social events and other functions. The DfES (2003a) describes how at one Secondary setting parents were provided with transport to facilitate attendance at such events as parents' evenings, concerts and reviews of Individual Educational Plans (IEPs).

For minority ethnic families to feel part of the educational setting, Stead et al. (1999) argue that there needs to be recognition of them in the learning environment. This can be achieved by using the following strategies:

- Be culturally sensitive.

- Display pictures of minority ethnic families around the classroom.

- Create a book with each page completed by an indiviudal family and displayed for others to read and reflect on.

- Make displays showing family and community members which can be used to form part of the Welcome board.

- Bring the local community, in which parents live and work, into the classroom.

Whilst all of the strategies above can be effective, many educationalists including Keyes (2002) and Wolfendale (1992) are keen to explore the value and use of the local community in supporting the education of minority ethnic pupils. The remainder of this chapter will explore this important area of focus and is intended to complement our earlier discussions in the book.

Working with the local community

The local community potentially offers a wealth of activity, innovation and support to enable schools and practitioners to work together through effective collaboration. Three key features of the local community will be explored including the use of local authorities, professional groups and outside agencies, and making effective links with the wider community.

Local Authorities (LAs)

LAs can offer practitioners and settings support and guidance, particularly relating to supporting asylum seeker and refugee and Gypsy, Roma and Traveller children and their parents. As each LA works in different ways, practitioners reading and reflecting on this are encouraged to contact key personnel in their LA, as they will be able to provide guidance, support and information relating to the following:

- Admission procedures.

- Teaching support.

- Co-ordination of the work of voluntary and statutory agencies.

- Initial assessments of pupils.

- Compilation of basic information and background details of families.

- Access to financial support.

Implications for future practice

- Make contact with your LA through various means, for example by telephone, email, letter.

- Speak *directly* to key personnel – advisors and support staff.

- Organize regular meetings with key personnel to support you – keep them informed of your progress and your needs.

- Ensure you have correct contact details – full names, times of availability and correct email addresses, telephone numbers and postal addresses.

Support can also be sought through extended school provision and Children's Centres. Discussions with your LA will develop your understanding of these important developments in education.

Professional groups and outside agencies

Whilst the LA can offer a level of support, practitioners and schools will also recognize that there is a wide range of professional groups, health and social services and voluntary agencies in each area that can offer support to professions and families by working collaboratively both inside and outside of the setting. (A list of possible contacts is provided in the appendices.)

Building up a local directory of individual agencies and inter-agency links will provide schools and families with an overview of the range of contacts available and their specific areas of expertise. This is a very useful strategy because it is important not to forget that to effectively work with parents we need to ensure that we are aware not only of their children's needs but also their family needs as well. This is clearly modelled in the case study below.

Case study

OFSTED (2003) describes the practice of one Primary setting, located near the centre of a Midlands city, which makes excellent provision for the needs of its newly arrived pupils and their parents. This is mostly established in the induction procedures used by the setting (highlighted in Chapter 2) during which:

■ An assessment of parental needs is made to facilitate integration into the community.

■ Access is provided to local doctors, dentists, clinics, legal services and, if required, co-ordinated medical services with expert doctors and psychological support for those children or parents subject to trauma and the effects of torture.

■ Invitations are made to parents' drop-in counselling centres both at the setting and at the local community centre.

Links with the wider community

Links with the wider community tend to be specific to each setting. Such links can be made with any of the following:

■ Neighbours in the vicinity.

■ Local shops and businesses – vets, shops, trade and commerce.

■ Places of religious worship.

■ Music, drama and dance groups.

■ Local action groups.

- The local media – press, television, radio.

- Local and national charities and organizations.

- Local police liaison officers.

An important link which many practitioners unfortunately overlook is that associated with supplementary schools. Largely run by voluntary local community groups in a variety of venues, supplementary schools provide a wealth of learning opportunities for many minority ethnic children at evenings and weekends (to learn more about the background of these schools and read about the associated strengths and weaknesses of these schools please visit www.continyou.org.uk/content.php?CategoryID=632).

To forge effective links with the community, it is also important for practitioners to make the 'first move' by going out of the setting to visit children at home and/or to use local shops and cafes. Other strategies include asking for invitations to families' churches, temples and social centres and discussing the possibility of holding meetings and exhibitions in the setting or in the community. The case study below explores this further.

Case Study – Bringing settings, parents and the local community together: Effective Partnerships with Parents (EPPa)

A four-year pilot in Devon, supported by the DfES, the Learning and Skills Council, three LAs and the National Confederation of PTAs, led to the formulation of an EPPa – a scheme for improving relationships between settings, parents and the local community. Johnstone (2004) explains how by setting up an Action Team the partnership managed to work on a range of projects, including the setting up of an internet 'buddy' scheme for pupils, parents and staff during transition periods between Primary and Secondary settings, training volunteers, and organizing family learning events and parenting workshops.

From the four-year pilot, a toolkit has been produced which provides the help and guidance to support practitioners in forming one of these EPPas. As Johnstone (2004: 16) states: 'EPPa is first and foremost a setting improvement tool. However, for settings wanting public recognition for their outstanding work with parents, EPPa also offers an optional award scheme.'

Also useful are the suggested readings below which will offer further support, advice and strategies to develop effective relationships and partnerships with parents and the local community.

- DfES (2002) 'Parent's Gateway' (online resource), available at www.dfes.gov.uk/parents gateway/index.shtml.

- Hughes, P. (2002) *Principles of Primary Education Study Guide* (2nd edition), London: David Fulton. (See Chapter 10 on home–setting–community connections.)

- Mills, J. (1996) *Partnership in the Primary Setting*. Abingdon: Routledge.

- Waller, H. and Waller, J. (1998) *Linking Home and Setting*. London: David Fulton.

Working with parents and the local community is a tremendously rewarding experience yet is at the same time arduous, particularly as 'practitioners are really the glue that holds home/setting partnerships together' (Patrikakou and Weissberg, 1999: 36, cited in Keyes 2002). It is therefore important to remember the main reason as to why these partnerships are developed – *for the good of the children you teach.*

Key Points

- There are a wealth of ways in which practitioners and settings can work together with minority ethnic parents to raise the academic achievement of their children, particularly those from an asylum seeker and refugee and Gypsy, Roma and Traveller background.

- There are a number of benefits from involving parents in their children's education.

- There are a number of reasons as to why parents, particularly those from a minority ethnic background, may not be involved in their child's education.

- Developing strong relationships with minority ethnic parents is essential practice.

- There are a number of different types of involvement parents can undertake with regard to their children's education.

- There is a range of links which can be made with the local community to help raise the academic attainment of minority ethnic children.

CHAPTER 7

Final thoughts

> There is a real sense that the time has come to address unflinchingly issues identified some thirty years ago (Hunte 2004: 36).

As we said at the outset of this book, under-achievement amongst minority ethnic groups is not a new phenomenon: we have known about this inequality for several decades (Coard 1971) and more recently government has responded with the Aiming High agenda (DfES 2003a). The focus of our book has been the role of teachers and trainees in helping pupils perform to their true potential. Our focus has been on specific groups which can be characterized by ethnicity and gender, namely, asylum seeker and refugee children, pupils who speak English as an additional language, Black African and Caribbean boys, Pakistani and Bangladeshi boys, and Gypsy, Roma and Traveller children in the UK. Other groups of learners, beyond the remit of this book, are also worthy of attention, for example 'looked after children', and those on 'free school meals'. Both of these groups have been identified in recent government reports as under-achieving (DfES 2006a). Similarly White, working-class boys and girls in some educational settings have been noted for poor attendance and low attainment.

However, a number of factors impact on this complex issue, so it is not just the quality of teaching within individual classrooms, but within a school and beyond: discriminatory school practices such as the exclusion rate of specific pupil groups; personal identity; and peer influence all impact on attainment (DfES 2006b). Constant updating of our professional knowledge and an awareness of the changing nature of cultural diversity in classrooms are required. Without these, practitioners cannot adequately respond to the needs of different learning groups and be informed of 'good practice' which has an application for all pupils.

REFERENCES

Ali, N. Kalra, V. S. and Sayyid, S. (eds) (2006) *A Postcolonial People: South Asians in Britain*. London: Hurst and Co.

Baker, R. (ed.) (1983) *The Psychological Problems of Refugees*. London: The Refugee Council.

Beveridge, S. (2005) *Children, Families and Schools*. Abingdon: RoutledgeFalmer

Bhopal, J. (2004) 'Gypsy travellers and education: changing needs and changing perceptions,' *British Journal of Educational Studies*, 52(1): 47–64.

Bhopal, K., Gundara, G., Jones, C. and Owen, C. (2000) *Working Towards Inclusive Education: Aspects of Good Practice for Gypsy and Traveller Pupils*. London: DfES

Birt, Y. (2001) *Being a Real Man in Islam: Drugs, Criminality and the Problem of Masculinity*. Available at http://homepage.ntlworld.com/masud.ISLAM/misc/drugs.htm

Blackledge, A. (2000) *Literacy, Power and Social Justice*. Stoke-on-Trent: Trentham.

Blair, M. (2001) *Why Pick on Me? School Exclusion and Black Youth*. Stoke-on-Trent: Trentham.

Bloom, B.S. (1956) *Taxonomy of Educational Objectives*. Susan Fauer Company Inc.

Bolloten, B. and Spafford, T. (2003) *Managing Mid-Phase Pupil Admissions: A Resource and Guidance Folder for Schools*. London: London Borough of Newham.

Brah, A. (1992) 'Difference, diversity and differentiation', in J. Donald and A. Rattansi (eds), *Race, Culture and Difference*. Buckingham: Open University.

Brent Language Service (1999) *Enriching Literacy – Text, Talk and Tales in Today's Classroom*. Stoke-on-Trent: Trentham.

Bridge, H. (2001) 'Increasing parental involvement in the pre-school curriculum: what an action research case study revealed', *International Journal of Early years Education*, 9 (1): 5–21.

Brown, K. (1965) *Social Psychology*. London: Macmillan.

Callendar, C. (1997) *Education for Empowerment: The Practice and Philosophies of Black Teachers*. Stoke-on-Trent: Trentham.

Children Now (2005) 'The culture of achievement', 19–25 January, 20-21.

Clark, C. and Greenfields, M. (2006) *Here to Stay: The Gypsies and Travellers of Britain*. Hatfield: University of Hertfordshire Press.

Coard, B. (1971) *How the West Indian Child is made Educationally Sub-normal in the British School System*. London: New Beacon.

Commission for Racial Equality (CRE) (2000) *Learning for All: Standards for Race Equality in Schools*. London: CRE.

Commission on the Future of Multi-Ethnic Britain (2000) *The Parekh Report*. London: Profile.

Connolly, P. (2003) *Boys and Schooling in the Early Years*, London: RoutledgeFalmer.

Cork, L. (2005) *Supporting Black Pupils and Parents: Understanding and Improving Home–School Relations*. Abingdon: Routledge.

Council of Europe (1972) *Selected Texts: The European Convention on Human Rights and Fundamental Freedoms*. Strasbourg: Council of Europe.

Crozier, G. (2001) 'Excluding parents: the deracialisation of parental involvement (1)', *Race, Ethnicity and Education*, 4 (4): 329–41.

Cummins, J. (1996) *Negotiating Identities: Education for Empowerment in a Diverse Society*. Covina, CA: California Association for Bilingual Education.

Cummins, J. and Scheker, S. (2003) *Multilingual Education in Practice: using diversity as a resource*. Portsmouth: Heinemann

Dadzie, S. (2000) *Toolkit for Tackling Racism in Schools*. Stoke-on-Trent: Trentham.

Demack, S., Drew, D. and Grimsley, M. (2000) 'Minding the gap: ethnic gender and social differences in attainment at 16', *Race, Ethnicity and Education*, 3 (2): 117–43.

Department for Education and Science (DES) (1967) *Children and their Primary Schools: The Plowden Report: Central Advisory Council for Education (England)*. London: HMSO.

Department for Education and Science (DES) (1975) *A Language for Life* (*The Bullock Report*). London: DfES.

Department for Education and Science (DES) (1985) *Education for all (The Swann Report)*. London: HMSO

Department for Education and Science (DES) (1989) *The National Curriculum*. London: DES.

Department for Education and Skills (DfES) (1998a) *National Literacy Strategy*. London: DfES.

Department for Education and Skills (DfES) (1998b) *National Numeracy Strategy*. London: DfES

Department for Education and Skills (DfES) (1999) *Curriculum Guidance for the Foundation Stage*. Norwich: DfES.

Department for Education and Skills (DfES) (2002) *The National Literacy Strategy: Supporting Pupils Learning English as an Additional Language* (Module 5). London: DfES.

Department for Education and Skills (DfES) (2003a) *Aiming High: Raising the Achievement of Minority Ethnic Pupils*. London: DfES.

Department for Education and Skills (DfES) (2003b) *Aiming High: Raising the Achievement of Gypsy and Traveller Pupils: A Guide to Good Practice*. London: HMSO.

Department for Education and Skills (DfES) (2004a) Aiming High: *Supporting the Effective use of Ethnic Minority Education Grant*. London: DfES.

Department for Education and Skills (DfES) (2004b) *Aiming High: Guidance on Supporting the Education of Asylum Seeker and Refugee Children*. London: DfES.

Department for Education and Skills (DfES) (2006a) *National Curriculum Assessment: GCSE Attainment and Equivalent Attainment and Post-16 Attendance by Pupil Characteristics 2005*. London: DfES.

Department for Education and Skills (DfES) (2006b) *Ethnicity and Education: The Evidence on Minority Ethnic Pupils aged 5–16*. Annesley, Nottingham: DfES.

Department for Education and Skills (DfES) (2006c) *Every Child Matters*. London: HMSO.

Department for Education and Skills (DfES) (2006d) *Excellence and Enjoyment: Planning and Assessment*. London: DfES.

Derby City Council (1999) 'Supporting New Arrivals with English as an Additional Language', (Draft 8/99). Available from The Access Service, Derby City Education Service, Middleton House, 27 St Mary's Gate, Derby DE1 3NN.

Derrington, C. (2005) Perceptions of behaviour and patterns of exclusion, *Journal of Research in Special Education Needs* 5 (2): 55–61.

DfE (1993) *Building Effective School–Business Links: a practical guide to improving quality*. London: DfE.

Driessen, G., Smit, F. and Sleegers, P. (2005) 'Parental involvement and educational achievement', *British Educational Research Journal*, 31 (4): 509–32.

Dufour, B. (1990) *A New Social Curriculum: A Guide to Cross-Curricular Issues*. Cambridge: Cambridge University Press.

Dyregrov, A. (1991) *Grief in Children*. London: Jessica Kingsley.

Edwards, V. (1998) *The Power of Babel: Teaching and Learning in Multilingual Classrooms*. Stoke-on-Trent: Trentham.

Epstein, D. (ed) (1990) *Failing Boys?: issues in gender and achievement*. Buckingham: Open University Press.

Fitzgerald, D. (2004) *Parent Partnerships in the Early Years*. London: Continuum.

Fletcher, S. (2000) *Mentoring in schools: a handbook of good practice*. London: Kogan Page.

Fuller, M. (1980) 'Black girls in a London comprehensive', in R. Deem (ed.), *Schooling for Women's Work*. London: Routledge and Kegan Paul.

Furedi, F. (1997) *Culture of Fear*. London: Cassell.

Gaine, C. (1987) *No Problem Here*. London: Hutchinson.

Gaine, C. (2005) *We're All White Thanks: The Persisting Myth about 'White' Schools*. Stoke-on-Trent: Trentham.

Gibbons, P. (2002) *Scaffolding Language, Scaffolding Learning: Teaching Second Language Learners in the Mainstream Classroom*. Oxford: Heinemann.

Gidden, A. (2001) *Sociology* (4th edition). Cambridge: Polity.

Gillborn, D. and Gipps, C. (1996) *Recent Research on the Achievements of Ethnic Minority Pupils*. London: HMSO.

Gillborn, D. and Mirza, H. S. (2000) *Educational Inequality: Mapping Race, Class and Gender*. London: OFSTED.

Guardian (2005) 'French unrest spreads', 8 November, 1.

Guardian (2006) 'French police criticised over the deaths of youths that led to the riots', 8 December, 28.

Guttman, A. (ed.) (1992) *Multiculturalism*. Chichester: Princeton University Press.

Hammond, J. (2001) *Scaffolding – Reading and Learning in Language and Literacy Education*. NSW, Australia: Primary English Teaching Association.

Herbert, C. (2003) *A PSHE and Citizenship Programme of Work for Key Stages 1 and 2*. London: Westminster Education Action Zone.

Hester, H. et al. (1993) *Guide to the Primary Learning Record*. Available from The Centre for Language in Primary Education, Webber Row, London.

HMSO (1981) *The Rampton Report: West Indian Children in our Schools*. London: HMSO.

Hughes, P. (2002) *Principles of Primary Education Study Guide* (2nd edition). London: David Fulton.

Hunte, C. (2004) 'Inequality, achievement and African-Carribean boys', *Race Equality Teaching*, 22 (3): 31-6.

Independent (2006a) 'Dress Sense', 16 October, 28.

Independent (2006b) 'Muslim veils should be illegal in public', 24 December, 6.

Johnstone, D. (2004) 'Put parents in charge', *Headteacher Update*, (Summer) 1, 4: 16.

Jordan, E. (2001) 'Exclusion of Travellers in state schools', *Educational Research*, 43 (2): 117–32.

Keyes, C. R. (2002) 'A way of thinking about parent/teacher partnerships for teachers', *International Journal of Early Years Education*, 10 (3): 177–91.

Kirsh, M. (2005) 'The Culture of Achievement' *Children Now*, 19–25 January, 20–21.

Klassen, N. and Clutterbuck, D. (2002) *Implementing Mentoring Schemes*. Oxford: Butterworth-Heinemann.

Knowles, E. and Ridley, W. (2006) *Another Spanner in the Works: Challenging Prejudice and Racism in Mainly White Schools*. Stoke-on-Trent: Trentham.

Kotler, A., Wegerif, R. and Levoi, M. (2002) 'Oracy and the Educational Achievement of Pupils with English as an Additional Language: The impact of bringing "Talking Partners" into Bradford schools', *Journal of Bilingual Education and Bilingualism*, 4(6).

Levinson, M. and Sparkes, A. (2003) 'Gypsy masculinities and the school–home interface: exploring contradictions and tensions', *British Journal of Sociology of Education*, 24 (5): 587–603.

London Development Agency (LDA) (2004) *Research Findings: The Educational Experience and Achievements of Black Boys in London Schools*. London: LDA.

Long, R. (1986) *Developing Parental Involvement in Primary Schools*. London: Macmillan Education.

Macauley, B. (2000) *Raising the attainment of Ethnic Minority Pupils – What Strategies are Recognised?* Stoke-on-Trent: Trentham.

Macbeth, A. (1989) *Involving Parents: Effective Parent–Teacher Relations*. Oxford: Heinemann.

MacPherson, W. (1999) *Report of an Inquiry by Sir William MacPherson of Cluny: The MacPherson Report (Inquiry into the death of Stephen Lawrence)*. London: HMSO.

Maiden, A. (2006) 'Hidden treasures', *Headteacher Update*, (Spring) 2 (2): 10.

Manchester City LEA (2001) *Welcome Pack*. Manchester: LEA.

Mazlow, A. (1954) *Motivation and Personality*. New York: Harper & Row.

McBride, B. A. and Rane, T.R. (1997) 'Father/male involvement in Early Childhood programs: issues and challenges', *Early Childhood Education Journal*. 25 (1): 11–15.

Miller, L., Cable, C, and Devereux, C. (2005) *Developing Early Years Practice*. London: David Fulton.

Mills, J. (1996) *Partnership in the Primary School*. London: Routledge.

Mirza, H. S. (1992) *Young, Female and Black*. London: Routledge.

Modood, T. (2003) 'Muslims and the politics of difference', in S. Spencer (ed.), *The Politics of Migration*. Oxford: Blackwell.

Modood, T., Berthoud, R., Lakey, J., Nazroo, J., Smilth, P., Virdee, S. and Beishon, S. (1997) *Ethnic Minorities in Britain:Diversity and Disadvantage*. London: Policy Studies Institute.

Modood, T. Triandafyllidou, A. and Zapata-Barrero, R. (2006) *Multicultural, Muslims and Citizenship: A European Approach*. London: Routledge.

Mouchel Parkman (2003)*Raising the Attainment of Black Boys*. Report prepared by L. Appiah for the DfES. Available from Mouchel Parkman Consultancy, West Hall, Parvis Road, West Byfleet, Surrey KT14 6EZ.

Munn, P. (ed.) (1993) *Parents and Schools: Customers, Managers or Partners?* London: Routledge.

Naidoo, J. (ed.) (2002) *Somali Children in our Schools*. London: Tower Hamlets Language Support Services.

O'Hanlon, C. and Homes, P. (2004) *The Education of Gypsy and Traveller Children: Towards Inclusion and Educational Achievement*. Stoke-on-Trent: Trentham.

OFSTED (1996a) *Recent Research on the Achievements of Ethnic Minority Pupils*. London: OFSTED.

OFSTED (1996b) *The Education of Travelling Children*. London: HMSO.

OFSTED (1999a) *Raising the Attainment of Minority Ethnic Pupils*. London: HMSO.

OFSTED (1999b) *Raising the Attainment of Minority Ethnic Pupils: Schools and LEA Responses*. London: OFSTED.

OFSTED (2001) *Managing Support for the Attainment of Pupils from Minority Ethnic Groups*. London: OFSTED.

OFSTED (2002a) *Achievement of Black Caribbean Pupils: Good Practice in Secondary schools*. London: HMSO.

OFSTED (2002b) *The Achievement of Black Caribbean Pupils: Three Successful Primary Schools*. London: HMSO.

OFSTED (2003) *The Education of Asylum-Seeker Pupils*. London: OFSTED.

Organisation for Co-operation and Developemnt (OECD) (1997) *Parents as Partners in Schooling*. Paris: OECD.

Parekh, B. (2000) *Rethinking Multiculturalism: Cultural Diversity and Political Theory*. Basingstoke: Macmillan.

Parker-Jenkins, M. (1995) *Children of Islam – A Teacher's Guide to Meeting the needs of Muslim pupils*. Stoke-on-Trent: Trentham.

Parker-Jenkins, M. and Haw, K. (1996) 'Equality within Islam not without it: The perspectives of Muslim girls', *Muslim Educational Quarterly*, 3: 17-34.

Parker-Jenkins, M., Hartas, D. and Irving, B. (2005) *In Good Faith: Schools, Religion and Public Funding*. Aldershot: Ashgate.

Pearce, S. (2005) *YOU Wouldn't Understand ... White Teachers in Multi-Ethnic Classrooms*. Stoke-on-Trent: Trentham

Pugh, G. and De'Ath, E. (1989) *Working Towards Partnership in the Early Years*. London: National Children's Bureau.

QCA (1999) *The National Curriculum*. London: QCA.

QCA (2000) *A Language In Common: Assessing English as an Additional Language*. London: QCA.

Rashid, N., Naz, I. and Hussain, M. (2005) *Raising attainment of Bangladeshi and Pakistani Boys (RAPBB): Project Report and Good Practice Guide*. Birmingham Advisory and Support Service (BASS).

Rattansi, A. (1992) 'Changing the subject? Racism, culture and education', in J. Donald and A. Rattansi (eds), *Race, Culture and Difference*. London: Sage.

Rattansi, A. (2000) 'On Being and Not Being Brown/Black British: Racism, Class, Sexuality and Ethnicity in Post-Imperial Britain', *Interventions*, vol. 2, issue 1, March, pp118–34.

Reay, D. (1998) *Class Work: Mothers' Involvement in their Children's Primary Schooling*. London: UC Press.

Refugee Council (1999) *The Refugee Resources in the UK: A National Directory of Services for Asylum-Seekers and Refugees*. London: RC Relations/Oxford: Heinemann Educational.

Refugee Council and Save the Children (2001) *In Safe Hands (a resource and training pack to support work with young refugee children)*. London: RC/Save the Children.

Reynolds, M., McCartan. M. and Knipe, D. (2003) 'Traveller culture and lifestyle as factors influencing children's integration into mainstream secondary schools in West Belfast', *International Journal of Inclusive Education*, 7 (4): 403–14.

Richardson, R. (2006) 'Race, identity and multiculturalism – the current debates', (notes for a talk, University of Derby, 1 March 2006).

Richardson R. and Wood, A. (2004) *The Achievement of British Pakistani Learners: Work in Progress*. (The Report of the RAISE project, 2002–4, funded by Yorkshire Forward.) Stoke-on-Trent: Trentham.

Richman, N. (1998) *In the Midst of the Whirlwind: A Manual for Helping Refugee Children*. Save the Children. Stoke-on-Trent: Trentham.

Riley, J. (1998) 'Curiosity and Communication: Language and Literacy in the Early Years Educators', in I. Siraj-Blatchford (ed.), *A Curriculum Development Handbook for Early Childhood*. Stoke-on-Trent: Trentham.

Rowan, L., Knobel, M., Bigum, C. and Lankshear, C. (2002) *Boys, Literacies and Schooling: the Dangerous Territories of Gender-Based Literacy*. Buckingham: Open University Press.

Runnymede Trust (1997) *Islamaphobia: A Challenge for Us All*. London: Runnymede.

Rutter, J. (1994) *Refugee Children in the Classroom*. Stoke-on-Trent: Trentham.

Rutter, J. (2001) *Supporting Refugee Children in 21st Century Britain: A Compendium of Essential Information*. Stoke-on-Trent: Trentham Books.

Rutter, J. and Jones, J. (1998) *Refugee Education: Mapping the Field*. Stoke-on-Trent: Trentham.

Sanders, T. (2004) 'Cat Have Two Mouses'. Paper contributed to *The Report of the RAISE project – The Achievement of British Pakistani Learners*. Stoke-on-Trent: Trentham.

Sarwar, G. (1994) *British Muslims and Schools*. Available from Muslim Educational Trust, 130 Stroud Green Road, London N4 3AZ.

Sewell, T. (1996) *Black Masculinities and Schooling*. Stoke-on-Trent: Trentham.

Sewell, T. (2007) *Generating Genius: Boys in Search of Love, Ritual and Schooling*. Stoke-on-Trent: Trentham.

Shah, M. (2001) *Working with Parents*. Oxford: Heinemann.

Sinfin Community School (2003) *Supporting New Arrivals in the Classroom*. Available from Language Support Department, Sinfin Community School, Farmhouse Road, Sinfin, Derby DE24 3AR.

Skelton, C. (2001) *Schooling the Boys: Masculinities and Primary Education*. Buckingham: Open University Press.

Smit, F., Driessen, G. and Sleegers, P. (2002) Parental Involvement and Educational Achievement. *British Educational Research Journal*, (August) 31 (4): 509–32

Smyth, G. (2002) *I Can't Read 'Rag' and 'Bug' – Bilingual Children's Creative Responses to a Monolingual Curriculum: Multicultural Teaching*. Stoke-on-Trent: Trentham Books.

Spafford, T. and Bolloten, B. (2001) 'Supporting refugee children in east London primary schools', in J. Rutter and C. Jones (eds), *Refugee Education: Mapping the Field*. Stoke-on-Trent: Trentham.

Spafford, T. et al. (1995) *The Admission and Induction of Refugee Children into School: Multicultural Teaching*, Stoke-on-Trent: Trentham.

Stacey, M. (1991) *Parents and Teachers Together*. Buckingham: Open University Press.

Stead, J., Closs, A. and Arshad, R. (1999) 'Invisible pupils: the experience of refugee pupils in Scottish schools', *Education and Social Justice*, 4: 49–55.

Teacher Training Agency (TTA) (2002) *Qualified Teacher Status*. London: TTA.

Times (2007) 'Reid set for tough new immigration rules', 26 January, 3.

Tizard, B. and Phoenix, A. (2002) *Black, White or Mixed Race: Race and Racism in the Lives of Young People of Mixed Parentage*. London: Routledge.

Tizard, B., Mortimore, J. and Burchell, B. (1981) *Involving Parents in Nursery and Infant Schools*. Suffolk: Grant McIntyre.

Tomlinson, S. (1991) *Home and school in multicultural Britain*. London: Batsford Academic and Educational.

Troyna, B. (1986) 'Beyond multiculturalism: towards the enactment of anti-racist education in policy, provision and pedagogy', *Oxford Review of Education*, 13: 22–36.

University of Derby (2006) 'Aim Higher Derbyshire', *Newsletter*. Available from Business Development Unit, University of Derby, Kedleston Road, Derby DE22 1GB.

Van Driel, B. (ed.) (2004) *Confronting Islamaphobia in Educational Practice*. Stoke-on-Trent: Trentham.

Vincent, C. and Ball, S.J. (2003) *Childcare choices and class practices*. London: Routledge.

Virani-Roper, Z. (2000) 'Bilingual learners and numeracy', in M. Gravelle (ed.), *Planning for Bilingual Learners*. Stoke-on-Trent: Trentham.

Vygotsky, L. (1962) *Thought and Language*. Cambridge, MA: MIT.

Waller, H. and Waller, J. (1998) *Linking Home and Setting*. London: David Fulton.

Weeks, D. and Wright, C. (1998) *Improving Practice: A Whole School Approach to Raising the Achievement of African Caribbean Youth*. London: The Runnymede Trust.

Wilce, H. (2006) *Complex tales of the males*. Times Educational Supplement, 7 July 2006. www.tes.co.uk/search/story/?story_id=2259419. Accessed 21 June 2007.

Wilkes, S. (1994) *One Day we had to Run!: Refugee Children tell their Stories in Words and Paintings*. London: Evans Brothers Ltd.

Williams-Ellis, A. (1973) *Gypsy folk tales*. London: Pan.

Wolfendale, S. (1992) *Empowering Parents and Teachers: Working for Children*. London: Cassell.

Wormington, A., Newman, S. and Lilly, C. (eds.) (2003) *The Travelling People*. London: Newham, Hackney and Tower Hamlets Education Services.

Wright, C. (1992) *Race Relations in the Primary School*. London: David Fulton

Wright, C., Weekes, D. and McGlaughlin, A. (2000) *'Race', Class and Gender in Exclusion from School*. London: Falmer Press.

Wright, M., Barge, J.K. and Loges, W.E. (2000) 'Parent, Student and Teacher Perceptions of Parental Involvement', *British Education Research Journal* 28 (3): 140–63.

Wrigley, T. (2000) *The Power to Learn: Stories of Success in the Education of Asian and other Bilingual Pupils*. Stoke-on-Trent: Trentham.

Zipes, J. (1976) *Fairy Tales and Urban Myths*. London

A range of resources and information can be found at the following websites:

100 Great Black Britons	www.100greatblackbritons.com
1001 Inventions	www.1001inventions.com
Active 8	www.nationwidechildcare.co.uk/activities8.htm
Amnesty International	www.amnesty.org
Asylum Aid	www.asylumaid.org.uk
Black and Asian History	www.channel4blackandasianhistory.
Black, Asian and Pakistani Vounteers Group	www.gos.gov.uk/goem
Boys 2 Men	www.fathersdirect.com
Braingym	www.learning-solutions.co.uk
Britkids	www.britkid.org
British Red Cross Society	www.redcross.org.uk
Centre for the Use of Research and Evidence in Education (CUREE)	www.curee-paccts.com/index.jsp
Commission for Racial Equality	www.cre.gov.uk
Criminal Records Bureau	www.crb.gov.uk
Department for Education and Skills.	www.dfes.org.uk
Derby City Council, Race Equality Policy	www.derby.gov.uk/primary
Development Education Association	www.dea.org.uk
DfES Anti-racist Teaching	www.insted.co.uk/raise.html
DfES Statistics/Pupil Performance	www.dfes.gov.uk/rsgateway
Ethiopian Community Association	www.ethiopiancommunity.co.uk
Eurokid	www.eurokid.org
European Council for Refugees and Exiles	www.ecre.org
European Convention on Human Rights and Fundamental Freedoms	www.hri.org/docs/ECHR50.html
Family Welfare Association	www.fwa.org.uk
From Boyhood to Manhood	www.usatfbmf.com
Generating Genius	www.generatinggenius.org.uk www.admin.ox.ac.uk

ICAR Information Centre about Asylum and Refugees in the UK	www.icar.org.uk
Immigration & Nationality Directorate of the Home Office	www.ind.homeoffice.gov.uk
Immigration Advisory Service	www.iasuk.org
Institute of Race Relations	www.irr.org.uk
Internal Displacement Project	www.idpproject.org
Joint Council for the Welfare of Immigrants	www.jcwi.org.uk
Law Centres Federation	www.lawcentres.org.uk
Liberty (National Council for Civil Liberties)	www.liberty-human-rights.org.uk
Migrant Helpline	www.migranthelpline.org.uk
Multiverse	www.multiverse.ac.uk
National Black Boys Can Association	www.blackboyscan.co.uk
National Coalition of Anti-deportation Campaigns	www.ncadc.org.uk
National Pupil Database	www.rlab.lse.uk/data/content/dataset
National Strategy	www.thegrid.org.uk/learning
North of England Refugee Centre	www.refugee.org.uk
Office for Standards in Education	www.ofsted.org.uk
Oxfam	www.oxfam.org.uk
Parents' Gateway	www.parentscentre.gov.uk/
Project Proactive	www.nottingham-schools.co.uk/goem
Pupil Level Annual School Census (PLASC)	www.schoolweb.gov.uk/locate/ management/ tar/plasc
QCA – Pathways to Learning for New Arrivals	www.qca.org.uk
Refugee Action	www.refugee-action.org.uk
Refugee Arrivals Project	www.refugee-arrivals.org.uk
Refugee Camp	www.refugeecamp.org
Refugee Council	www.refugeecouncil.org.uk
Refugee Housing Association	www.refugeehousing.org.uk
Refugee Studies Centre	www.rsc.ox.ac.uk
Refugee Women's Legal Group	www.rwlg.org.uk
Refugees Online	www.refugeesonline.org.uk
Reporting and Analysis for Improvement through School Self-Evaluation (RAISE online)	www.raiseonline.org
Respect Campaign	www.respect.gov.uk
Save the Children	www.scfuk.org.uk
Scottish Refugee Council	www.scottishrefugeecouncil.org.uk
Standards in Schools	www.standards.gov.uk/parentalinvolvement

Supplementary Education	www.continyou.org.uk/content.php?CategoryID=632
Talking Partners	www.educationbradford.com
Teacher Training Agency	www.tta.gov.uk
The ESRC Teaching and Learning Research Programme	www.tlrp.org
UNHCR (UN Refugee Agency)	www.unhcr.ch
United Nations Status of Refugees	www1.umn.edu/humanrts/instree/vlcrs.htm.
Welsh Refugee Council	www.welshrefugeecouncil.org

Useful contacts

National Asylum-Seekers Support Service
Home Office
Voyager House
30 Wellesley Road
Croydon
CRO 2AD

Refugee Legal Centre
Sussex House
Bermondsey Street
London
SEI 3XF

Refugee Support Centre
47 Lambeth Road
London
SW8 1RH

The Resource Unit for Supplementary
and Mother Tongue Schools
15 Great St Thomas Apostle
Mansion House
London
EC4V 2BB

INDEX